Take Back Our Party

Also by James Kwak

Economism

White House Burning (with Simon Johnson)

13 Bankers (with Simon Johnson)

Take Back Our Party:

Restoring the

Democratic Legacy

JAMES KWAK

STRONG
ARM
PRESS

Washington, DC

Interior Design: Jordan Jones, Coyote Arts LLC

ISBN   Paper: 978-1-947492-43-1
        E-Book: 978-1-947492-44-8

Strong Arm Press
www.strongarmpress.com
Washington, D. C.

For Willow and Henry,

that they may live in a more just world

than this one

Contents

The test of our progress is not whether we add more to the abundance of those who have much; it is whether we provide enough for those who have too little.
—Franklin Roosevelt, 1937

Introduction

Which side are you on?
— Florence Reece, 1931

We live in troubled times.

Ordinary Americans are struggling. Despite decades of technological innovation and economic growth, the typical family's net worth is no higher than in the 1980s.[1] Health care costs, including rising insurance premiums, deductibles, co-payments, prescription drug prices, and often unexpected out-of-network charges, bankrupt a growing number of once-secure families. Young adults are burdened by student loan payments extending as far as they can see. Steeply rising rents make finding an affordable home virtually impossible in more and more cities. State and local governments are failing to deliver even essential services like clean water to their residents. A handful of companies controlled by billionaires have levels of control over our lives once imaginable only in science fiction. Increasingly precarious federal government finances threaten future reductions in the Social Security and Medicare benefits that many elderly Americans rely on. And decades of unsustainable growth have already profoundly changed the climate of our planet in ways we are only now beginning to realize.

Yet despite these disturbing developments, many people—particularly those who are well-off and well-educated—insist that nothing could be better. As of 2019, the United States is in the 11th year of an economic expansion that has seen the stock market rise and the unemployment rate fall to record levels. We remain enthralled by every year's new marvels produced by the dream factories of the technology superpowers—self-driving cars, drone deliveries to your doorstep, virtual reality, space travel, and on and on. (The full realization of these wonders always seems just out of reach, but no matter.)

The explanation for this divergence is simple. Over the past 40 years, the economic fortunes of the very rich and more or less everyone else have become completely uncoupled. From 1980 to 2014, the total incomes of the top 1 percent more than tripled, while those of the bottom 50 percent remained essentially unchanged. The previous 34 years, from 1946 to 1980, saw the opposite pattern: Income growth was substantially higher for the bottom 50 percent than for the top 1 percent.[2] If you have the money, you live in one economy, with the best health care in the world, easy access to green space, the finest restaurants that have ever existed, elite educational institutions from preschool through the most opulent research universities anywhere, and luxury goods and services that once were reserved for royalty. If you don't have the money, you live in another economy, where your family's welfare is vulnerable to sudden changes in the demand for your skills generated by distant markets, you breathe the dirty air produced by uncontrolled development or drink the toxic water delivered by a crumbling infrastructure, your children go to underfunded public schools, and you are rapidly being priced out of the health care your family needs.

Obviously there is no border wall that cleanly divides the very rich from everyone else. There is an intermediate zone, roughly from the 75th to the 95th income percentile, where people are more or less comfortable in a material sense. But they can see the speed with which the truly wealthy have separated themselves from the rest of society, and many of them are desperate not to be left behind—if not for themselves, then for their children. Anxiety about getting into a good college, landing choice summer internships, and securing a job at one of the handful of highly selective companies that promise entry into the economic elite—Goldman Sachs, McKinsey, Google, Facebook, Amazon, and their few peers—is at pathological levels. The recent college admissions cheating scandal is not only more proof that the very rich live in a different world from everyone else, but also shows that they, too, are desperate to place their children on the educational escalator to success and fortune. The forward march of inequality is there for anyone to see, and no one wants his or her family to be caught on the wrong side of history.

This divide between the vast majority of Americans, who face the prospect of negligible improvements in their living standards at the cost of constant insecurity, and a small minority who both literally and figuratively jet away into another world, is the central economic challenge of our time. It is a problem in clear view today. Only one in five Americans think that today's youth will have a better life than their parents' generation—stark skepticism about what for centuries we have been calling the American dream.[3]

Inequality is a problem that, on its own, will only get worse. Technological advances will vastly increase the advantages of being rich and well-educated and the costs of not being so fortunate. Increasingly capable machines will displace low-skilled workers—consider how apps and kiosks are doing the job of cashiers at casual restaurants and big-box stores—while enriching the people who design them and the shareholders of the companies that manufacture them. Artificial intelligence will replace many knowledge workers while rewarding a small elite of computer scientists and their employers. It is true that people made the same doomsday predictions about earlier inventions, and in past ages of capitalism the market found higher-value occupations for many workers (though not necessarily for those who lost their jobs to new technology). It is possible that a society could adapt to these transformations in ways that help everyone, not just an intellectual and economic elite. But there is little reason to think that ours is such a society. In trusting to markets to allocate all good things, we have allowed the benefits of automation to be monopolized by people with the capital to invest in new technology and those with the skills to master it.

This is not merely an economic problem. It is hard to see how a society can long endure when the precarious fortunes, interests, and life experiences of its people become foreign to a small ruling class. ("Let them eat cake," a noblewoman in 18th-century France is reputed to have said upon hearing that the peasants had no bread.) The rise and fall of nations depend on the extent to which their economic and political institutions remain open to a wide range of interest groups within society, as documented by Daron Acemoglu and James Robinson in decades of research. Fourteenth-century Venice was both a democracy of sorts and a thriving commercial center of the Mediterranean. Once political power was seized by a closed hereditary aristocracy, however, the city-state fell into irreversible economic decline, eventually becoming the sinking museum that it is today.[4]

In a modern democracy, this should not happen—at least in theory. When everyone has an equal vote, a tiny minority of the super-rich should not be able to run away with the lion's share of society's economic gains. In the classical model, there should be a party of business and a party of labor, generally representing the rich and working class, respectively. The United States has never had a true labor party, but through the middle of the 20th century these roles were more or less approximated by Republicans and Democrats. The Republicans were the party of business, generally favoring lower taxes, smaller government, and fiscal responsibility. The Democrats were the party of labor unions and immigrant minorities, favoring higher taxes, bigger government, and more generous social programs. In the 1930s, it was Democratic President Franklin Roosevelt who established the federal safety net with public jobs programs and Social Security. In the 1960s, it was another Democratic president, Lyndon Johnson, who created Medicare and Medicaid, the last major expansions of the welfare state, and launched an optimistic "war on poverty."

During the past half-century, however, the tectonic plates of the political landscape have completely shifted. It is common knowledge that the Republican Party has been taken over by radical conservatives who want to dismantle government altogether (or, as Grover Norquist famously said, "reduce it to the size where I can drag it into the bathroom and drown it in the bathtub"[5]) and hold a host of unsavory views on immigration, racial and ethnic diversity, and women's rights. The parallel transformation of the Democratic Party has received relatively less attention. Today's Democratic elite—represented by Bill Clinton, Barack Obama, and Hillary Clinton—has, in deed if not in word, repudiated the heritage of Roosevelt and Johnson, fleeing what it sees as an embarrassing legacy peopled by unionized workers and welfare recipients. Instead, today's establishment Democrats style themselves as expert managers of a sophisticated market economy, friends of big finance and big technology, and architects of growth and opportunity. Instead of a party of capital and party of labor, the United States today has two parties of capital—one insular and "white nationalist," the other generally tolerant and multicultural[6]—or, as the pathbreaking economist Thomas Piketty has argued, two parties that represent different segments of the elite.[7] When it comes to economic policy, one is absolutist and ideological, the other technocratic and evidence-based, but both see growth as the overriding objective and markets as the optimal way to produce and distribute goods and services.

This is the political context that made it possible for the 1 percent to reach economic escape velocity and launch themselves away from the mundane, stagnant, anxiety-ridden lives of everybody else. The Democratic Party is dominated by people who fear nothing more than being called "liberals" (let alone "socialists") or being seen as soft-hearted, soft-headed believers in big government and the welfare state. Since the 1990s, the party's economic platform has been that markets deliver prosperity, and the role of government should be limited to correcting "market failures" such as externalities, adverse selection, or moral hazard, in the academic jargon employed by the policy elite. This is why Bill Clinton's lasting economic policy achievement was the introduction of work requirements for poverty assistance; this is why the greatest financial crisis in 70 years did not lead to structural change in the banking sector; this is why the health care program that bears Barack Obama's name is a warmed-over version of the plan introduced by Mitt Romney in Massachusetts, which was originally the brainchild of the reflexively conservative Heritage Foundation. As Republicans have succumbed to tribalism and irrationality, Democrats have claimed the mantle of fiscal prudence and responsible stewardship of the capitalist market economy.

The consequence is that the Democratic Party of the past 25 years has done next to nothing about inequality and has little to say about it. The party establishment has only taken up progressive policy ideas, such as the $15 minimum wage, when forced to by activists, usually working at the state or local level. The onetime defenders of the working class have stood idly by as the 1 percent has swept up an increasing share of the gains from economic growth, including the benefits of the post-recession recovery.[8] Its response has been to lecture that a rising tide lifts all boats—a maxim that differs little from the "trickle-down economics" so dear to conservatives. (Nominating Barack Obama for president at the 2012 Democratic National Convention, Bill Clinton acknowledged that too many people did not yet feel the effects of economic growth—but, he promised, "if you will renew the president's contract, you will feel it."[9]) Alternatively, Democrats will claim that some bundle of clever, market-friendly policies—funding for infrastructure spending and incentives for clean-technology investment are the current darlings—will magically shift the distribution of income and wealth down toward the working and middle classes.

Of course, the rise of inequality and the stagnation of the middle class are more the fault of the conservatives who took over the Republican Party than of the moderates who responded by shifting the Democratic Party to the political center. It is crucial to understand the conservative movement in order to appreciate how we got ourselves into our current mess. I have written books that were largely about Republicans—about their campaign to deregulate the financial sector, their willingness to sacrifice two centuries of fiscal responsibility on the altar of tax cuts, and their use of simplistic economic theories to mask policies that favor the rich.

But I am not a Republican and, if you are reading this, you probably aren't, either. More to the point, we can be certain that today's Republican Party—dominated as it is by ultra-wealthy donors and a fundamentalist ideology of cutting taxes for the rich and eliminating programs for everyone else—will do nothing to stem the rising tide of inequality or improve the economic fortunes of ordinary families. If we are going to more fairly share the vast wealth that our society produces, we first need a political party dedicated to improving the economic well-being of all Americans. That means we have to restore the historical identity of the Democratic Party as the champion of the poor, workers, and the middle class.

And so, because this is a book about how to make things better, it's a book about Democrats. It's about how, in the wake of the Reagan Revolution, we latched onto the idea that a more modern, more sophisticated, more business-friendly Democratic Party could successfully compete for the White House. It's about how this transformation, while paying off in victories in four of the past seven presidential elections (six if you go by the popular vote), has left us impotent in the face of growing inequality, even when in power, and incapable of making the case that we can help families struggling against economic insecurity and misfortune. And it's about how a new Democratic Party, dedicated to a progressive economic agenda, can take up the challenge of ensuring a decent life for every American.

CHAPTER 1

Their Democratic Party

Our New Choice plainly rejects the old categories and false alternatives they impose.... Liberal or conservative—the truth is, it's both, and it's different.
> —Bill Clinton, at the 1991 annual conference of the Democratic Leadership Council[10]

I have a poor memory of my own life, but I remember where I was when Bill Clinton was elected president: Kroeber Hall, on the campus of the University of California, Berkeley, in the evening of November 3, 1992. A friend and I were listening to the radio on a boombox when we heard the news. The nightmare of the Reagan-Bush years was over. We hugged. The Democrats were back in power.

Not surprisingly, I learned my politics from my parents. They came to the United States from South Korea, as they say, in search of a better life. My father arrived in San Francisco in 1953 on a freight ship that returned to America after delivering food to GIs fighting the Korean War. He then took a train and a bus across the country, arriving at Wesleyan University two months after the semester started (never having received the letter from Wesleyan telling him it was too late to come). My mother came nine years later to study at the University of Michigan. From them I learned that the Democrats were the party of workers, unions, and the poor, while the Republicans were the party of business and the rich.

The archetypal Democratic hero at the time was Franklin Roosevelt, the president of the New Deal, which included massive public works projects to fight unemployment, comprehensive regulation of the financial system, and the creation of Social Security. In 1944, he called for a "second Bill of Rights," which would guarantee all Americans a job, basic material necessities, housing, health care, and an education—but which never materialized. His successor, Harry Truman, proposed a universal, single-payer health care program. And in 1964, President Lyndon Johnson declared "unconditional war" on poverty, pushing forward a legislative agenda that included Medicare, Medicaid, food stamps, and federal subsidies for schools with poor children. That was what the Democratic brand still meant in the 1970s, when I was a child.

At that moment, however, the legacy of the New Deal was in danger, weakened by the Vietnam War and economic stagnation. With a growing backlash against regulation, high taxes, and the civil rights movement, the modern American conservative movement—which had languished in obscurity as recently as the 1950s—was poised to take over the Republican Party and then the country.

Democrats were aware that President Johnson's anti-poverty platform was losing viability on the national level. Jimmy Carter represented an alternative to traditional liberalism, but he was soundly rejected by voters in 1980 in favor of Ronald Reagan, who gave off an aura of breezy confidence that lower taxes and smaller government would unleash the American innovative spirit and usher in a new age of prosperity.

The reality of the Reagan Revolution, with its tax cuts for the rich and assault on the welfare state, was the fulfillment of Democrats' worst nightmares. After 12 years of Reagan and George H. W. Bush, we were desperate for change.

The change that Clinton represented, however, went beyond a simple partisan shift in the White House. His historical significance lay in what he did not do. He did not reverse the conservative revolution and restore the core values of the New Deal. Instead, Clinton signaled something far more important: a realignment of the traditional account of American politics, in which Democrats represented wage workers and Republicans represented executives and business owners. Things were never quite so simple, of course—Democrats had long been financially dependent on particular segments of the business class, increasingly throughout the 1980s—but in general terms the economic identities of the two parties were clear.

The Clinton election was a crucial turning point in a transformation of the Democratic Party that has lasted to this day, more than a quarter of a century later. As the Republicans shifted to the right, metamorphosing from perfunctory defenders of corporate America to rabid zealots for unregulated markets and minimal government, the Democrats followed in their wake. The party that was once our country's closest approximation to social democrats instead became technocratic cheerleaders for the market economy. Democratic politicians abandoned government policies that directly aided the disabled, the unlucky, and the poor, consoling themselves with the idea that facilitating overall economic growth was the best way to help the less fortunate.

The Clinton nomination in 1992 was itself the end product of a concerted effort to move the Democratic Party away from the left, with its embarrassing baggage of welfare programs and labor unions, and toward a more modern center. In the public's mind, Republicans had successfully portrayed their opponents as tax-and-spend liberals who suppressed individual initiative, gave handouts to welfare queens, coddled criminals, and appeased Communists. Instead of trying to stand up for the social safety net and progressive taxes (and a humane criminal justice system), many Democratic leaders and strategists chose to distance themselves from their liberal past, accepting the conservative caricature of the New Deal and its legacy. The new Democratic Party would be responsible with the nation's finances, strong on national defense, tough on crime, friendly to business, unfriendly to unions (except at election time), and supportive of free markets. In other words, it would be a lot like the Republican Party—but somehow, drawing on the credit it had built up from the 1930s through the 1960s, it would still claim to be the party of ordinary people.

The shift toward a market-centric ideology was foreshadowed by President Carter's 1980 re-election campaign, as he unsuccessfully tried to co-opt Reagan's vocabulary of individual initiative and freedom. "Every day millions of economic decisions are made in factories, in automobile showrooms, in banks and in brokerage houses, on farms and around kitchen tables ... according to private needs and private individual judgments," he said, attempting to rebut the charge that Democrats represented government control over the economy.[11] Pressure to move the party to the right increased after Carter's stinging loss (and the loss of the Senate majority for the first time since the Eisenhower administration). Louisiana Representative Gillis Long, the new chair of the House Democratic Caucus, sponsored the creation of a new Committee on Party Effectiveness, staffed notably by Al From. This committee began formulating a new platform—one focused on increasing private-sector competitiveness, reducing government spending, fighting inflation, and strengthening national defense. "We want to move away from a temporary economic policy of redistribution ... to a long-term policy of growth and opportunity," Representative Tim Wirth told reporters in 1982.[12]

The takeover of the party began in earnest, however, after President Reagan routed Democratic nominee Walter Mondale in the 1984 presidential election, which, many people thought, demonstrated the impotence of traditional liberalism (despite the fact that Mondale had promised higher taxes to reduce the national debt). Only weeks after the election, a group of major Democratic fundraisers met to discuss "how they might use their fund-raising skills to move the party toward their business-oriented, centrist viewpoints." The same month, at an event held by the centrist Coalition for a Democratic Majority, Governors Bruce Babbitt of Arizona and Charles Robb of Virginia rejected the New Deal and emphasized the need for the party to embrace the business community.[13] In 1985, former Caucus Committee director Al From founded the Democratic Leadership Council, which repudiated the populist economic agenda inherited from Roosevelt and Johnson in favor of market-based solutions that could broaden the party's appeal to the upper middle class and corporate America.

"We cannot afford to become a liberal party," From wrote in a memo for Long; "our message must attract moderates and conservatives, as well."[14] Their new message was a paean to growth and opportunity. "The private sector, not government, is the primary engine for economic growth," From wrote later. "Government's proper role is to foster private sector growth and to equip every American with the opportunities and skills that he or she needs to succeed in the private economy."[15] The DLC was one of the central institutions of what came to be known as the New Democrats, who distinguished themselves from the presumably "old" Democrats by staking out moderate or conservative—that is, Republican—positions on issues like defense spending, crime, inflation, budget deficits, and free trade. The Progressive Policy Institute, a think tank spun off from the DLC, even adopted one of the conservatives' favorite attack lines, arguing that the minimum wage harmed poor people by raising prices.[16]

In 1990, Arkansas Governor Bill Clinton became chair of the DLC. He later wrote in his memoir, "the so-called New Democrat philosophy ... was the backbone of my 1992 campaign for President."[17] Clinton spent his term as chair promoting the key themes of economic growth, limited government, and personal responsibility around the country— particularly in key primary states—before officially announcing his presidential candidacy in October 1991. He was joined on the campaign trail by Bruce Reed, former DLC policy director, who later became head of the president's Domestic Policy Council; Robert Shapiro, who moved from the Progressive Policy Institute to become a campaign adviser and later an undersecretary in the Commerce Department; and, of course, vice-presidential nominee Al Gore, a longtime DLC stalwart. After the election, Al From headed domestic policy on the transition team; DLC vice chair Mike Espy was named secretary of agriculture; and DLC member Lloyd Bentsen became Treasury secretary.

In many ways, Clinton was the perfect standard bearer for the New Democrats. He was a Southern governor, apparently unstained by the corruption of the big city or of Congress. He had an impressive reputation as a policy wonk, having won a Rhodes Scholarship and graduated from the Yale Law School. He could fly back to Arkansas during the campaign to order the execution of the mentally disabled Ricky Ray Rector to demonstrate how "tough on crime" he was. He emphasized welfare reform and school choice to highlight his willingness to break with past orthodoxies. He openly rejected his own party: "The choice we offer is not conservative or liberal. In many ways, it is not even Republican or Democratic," he said, accepting the nomination of the *Democratic Party.*[18]

And yet, in public, Clinton played as a populist. He promised opportunity for a middle class that "worked hard and played by the rules." His optimistic post-partisan rhetoric papered over the fact that many of his substantive positions—tax cuts, smaller government, welfare limits, increased policing, charter schools, and so on—were taken straight from Republicans. He was campaigning during the aftermath of a mild recession, promising jobs and health care. More importantly, he could act like a man of the people and, like no one else, he could feel your pain. President Clinton sustained that magic throughout his eight years in the White House. As his policies became more and more firmly anchored in the center, his personal charisma and political gifts preserved his image as a defender of the common man.

Two decades later, Democrats' memories of the Clinton administration tend to retain the Monica Lewinsky scandal, eight years of uninterrupted economic expansion, and little else. But in that period, Clinton put his stamp on the identity of his party like no president since Franklin Roosevelt.

Because he wanted to be all things to all people, Clinton won the 1992 election promising not just welfare reform but also a middle-class tax cut, health care reform, and more jobs. Even before his inauguration, however, his economic team sat him down and explained that his top priority would have to be not programs aimed at ordinary Americans, but ... the bond market. On January 7, 1993, the president-elect held a meeting with his economic team in Little Rock, Arkansas. According to his advisers—including Robert Rubin, former co-chairman of Goldman Sachs and Clinton's choice as director of the National Economic Council—Wall Street was concerned about the large budget deficits incurred by Republican tax cuts and spending increases. Investors were demanding high interest rates to buy Treasury bonds, which raised rates throughout the economy, making it harder for businesses and households to borrow and constraining growth.

The solution was to reduce budget deficits, which would lower interest rates and encourage more economic activity. Clinton supposedly responded, "You mean to tell me that the success of the program and my reelection hinges on the Federal Reserve and a bunch of fucking bond traders?"[19] But he sided with the bond market, giving up his hoped-for domestic programs for a package of tax increases and deficit reduction targets. The bill squeaked through Congress and helped fuel the Republicans' sweeping victories in the 1994 midterm elections.

In retrospect, there are arguments in favor of the 1993 tax increase. It did reduce budget deficits, interest rates did fall, and the economy did expand for the next seven years. By the time Clinton left office, the federal government was actually running a surplus on an annual basis. Still, it is impossible to definitively say what policy produced what macroeconomic outcome; interest rates were already falling, and the economy had already begun growing in March 1991.

It is clear, however, that the decision to focus on deficits left a lasting imprint on the identity of the Democratic Party. The economic boom of the 1990s—the longest in modern American economic history at the time—and the budget surpluses of Clinton's second term allowed his party to claim the high ground when it came to fiscal rectitude and macroeconomic management. In the past, Democrats had been big spenders, willing to shove money at the nation's problems, while Republicans had been the mature adults worrying about deficits. Now the tables were turned. The Republican Party was in the hands of conservatives who cut taxes at every opportunity, fervently insisting that deficits would require spending cuts in the future. By contrast, Clinton and his successors could claim to be the prudent, responsible ones who understood how the economy worked. This is why Democrats have objected to every Republican tax cut on the grounds that it would increase deficits, and why Barack Obama made a "grand bargain" to reduce the national debt a top political priority, even while the economy was struggling to recover from the Great Recession.

Clinton remained determined to follow through on his campaign promise of health care reform. One challenge was that he and his team (led by Hillary Clinton), wary of undermining their newfound credibility as deficit fighters, insisted that their plan had to be budget-neutral and could not require additional new taxes beyond those in the 1993 budget bill. Perhaps more important, they rejected the basic model proposed by earlier generations of Democrats: a universal, single-payer health insurance program similar to Medicare.

Instead, they were convinced that managed market competition, not a new government entitlement, could provide the solution to America's health care problems. Under the Clinton plan, consumers would choose their insurance from among plans offered by private insurers, either via large employers or via regional health alliances. Competition, the argument went, would give insurers the incentive to deliver superior health plans at reasonable prices, and insurers would then put pressure on providers to ensure quality and control costs. There are many reasons why health care reform suffered an ignominious defeat in Congress, never even coming up for a vote. The episode, however, was another landmark in the shift of the Democratic Party toward market-based, technocratic policies and away from the New Deal blueprint of large-scale government social programs.

The political backlash to the Clinton tax increase and health care debacle was overwhelming and immediate: The 1994 midterm elections gave Republicans control of both houses of Congress for the first time since the 1950s. The president's response was to double down on "triangulation"—staking out a third position on the political landscape distinct from both Democrats and Republicans. And so it was Clinton, a Democratic president, who announced in his 1996 State of the Union address that "The era of big government is over."[20] What began as a clever strategy to secure re-election in the wake of the crushing midterm defeat has since become the standard playbook of the party: splitting the difference between conservative Republicans and a caricature of a liberal Democratic base whose primary function is to make the party establishment seem reasonable by comparison. In most cases, triangulation has led to the adoption of positions once characteristic of moderate Republicans.

One way to seek out the middle was to enact tough-on-crime bills, including the Violent Crime Control and Law Enforcement Act of 1994, which increased funding for police and prisons while lengthening sentences for federal crimes, and the Antiterrorism and Effective Death Penalty Act of 1996, which virtually eliminated the ability of the federal courts to review state court decisions, particularly in death penalty cases. After 1994, the Clinton administration's only significant contribution to tax policy was a handout to the rich: the reduction in the maximum tax rate on capital gains from 28 percent to 20 percent in 1997. (Capital gains are the profits realized from selling assets, and thus are mainly collected by the wealthy.) Another of the president's meager economic policy achievements was the ratification and implementation of the North American Free Trade Agreement. Although the effects of NAFTA on the American economy were relatively slight, it helped Democrats distance themselves from their traditional roots in labor unions while ingratiating themselves with the business community and burnishing their image as advocates of free trade. And it led to more aggressive trade actions, like establishing permanent normal trade relations with China, which had a far more disastrous impact on the nation's industrial base, responsible for an 18 percent reduction in manufacturing employment from 2001 to 2007.[21]

At the core of the New Democrats' agenda was disassociating their party from the welfare state. Since the 1960s, conservatives had criticized government assistance programs for undermining personal responsibility and encouraging dependency on the state. By the 1980s, association with welfare was an enormous political weakness for Democrats. Republicans successfully popularized the image of the "welfare queen" and tarred Democrats as soft-hearted, weak-minded liberals who raised taxes on people who worked to fund lavish benefits for people who didn't. In

1984, Charles Murray's hugely influential book *Losing Ground* (written with funding from two conservative think tanks, the Manhattan Institute and the Heritage Foundation) argued that welfare programs harmed poor people by undermining their incentive to work.

Instead of defending the social safety net, the New Democrats simply co-opted the issue, adopting the idea that the poor needed better incentives to participate in the labor market. In 1986, DLC chair Charles Robb called for "a social policy that rewards self-discipline and hard work, not one that penalizes individual initiative."[22] In his 1992 campaign, Clinton staked out a position well to the right of President Bush, promising to "end welfare as we know it" and to impose a new work requirement that would kick in after two years of government assistance. In a 1993 interview, Clinton said, "[Murray's] analysis is essentially right," although he did not necessarily agree with the author's policy prescriptions.[23]

Once in office, Clinton backed his words with action. After his own welfare reform proposal fizzled out, the 1994 elections gave the initiative to congressional Republicans. While the president attacked some of their more extreme proposals, his administration quietly signaled his openness to a bill that he eventually signed into law as the Personal Responsibility and Work Opportunity Reconciliation Act of 1996 (an Orwellian name even by Washington standards).[24] As promised, the act completely transformed the welfare system. It eliminated Aid to Families with Dependent Children, which had ensured a federal entitlement to cash support, and replaced it with Temporary Assistance for Needy Families, a new program that allocated money as block grants to states, which could spend it more or less however they wished. (The block grants were also designed to decline over time, after accounting for inflation.) PRWORA set a lifetime maximum of five years of welfare support from federal funds and placed work requirements on recipients, while giving states the latitude to impose their own, more onerous restrictions. This "welfare to work" bill also included severe cuts to food stamp benefits and, in a premonition of worse things to come, cut off most legal immigrants from both food stamps and Supplemental Security Income (paid to the disabled and the very poor elderly).

Politically, welfare reform paid off handsomely. Clinton followed through on a 1992 campaign promise just in time for re-election while neutering a potent Republican attack line. By breaking with much of his own party (PRWORA was passed mainly with Republican votes, while congressional Democrats were roughly evenly split), the president perfectly executed the triangulation strategy, distinguishing himself from both poles of the political system. Or, as Republican presidential nominee Bob Dole put it, "By selling out his own party, Bill Clinton has proven he is ideologically adrift."[25] At the same time, by vetoing two earlier, more conservative bills, Clinton could still claim to be the protector of the downtrodden—or, at least, not as bad as the Republicans. He swept to victory over Dole just a few months later, while the balance of power in Congress remained virtually unchanged—seeming to demonstrate the benefits of running to the middle and portraying both liberals and conservatives as out of touch with America.

Welfare reform signaled that the Democrats were no longer the party of handouts to the poor. Instead of cash, the New Democrats promised to provide opportunity, which meant giving people the education necessary to compete in the new economy. Not surprisingly, President Clinton saw market incentives as the key to improving the public-school system. He embraced the idea of accountability, which was euphemistic shorthand for making the educational market more competitive. His administration supported nationwide K-12 standards and a requirement that states turn around or close schools that failed to meet those standards—in theory, a way to mimic the competitive forces of capitalism. The president also endorsed the budding charter school movement, which sought to provide a new source of competition to traditional public schools, which would be forced to improve or risk losing their students to the new entrants. The Federal Charter School Program, created in 1994, provided funds to support the development of charter schools by states and towns.

When it came to higher education, President Clinton helped launch the Federal Direct Student Loan Program, under which the government lends directly to students, instead of subsidizing and guaranteeing loans made by banks (thereby ensuring them risk-free profits). This was a small step in the right direction, but the focus on loan programs typified the New Democrats' approach to education. Instead of thinking of a college education as something that an advanced society should provide to its citizens, they saw it as an individual's private investment in her human capital; the government's role was simply to provide a nudge to make that investment easier to finance. At the same time, the Higher Education Amendments Act of 1998 made it more difficult to discharge student loans in bankruptcy. While this provision may have caused banks to lower interest rates on student loans (because they now faced less risk of not being paid back), it also had the effect of punishing those people who were unable to turn their college studies into higher-paying jobs.

With welfare reform and education policy, the New Democrats repudiated the vocabulary of social solidarity and economic security in favor of their cherished themes of opportunity, accountability, and competitiveness. But to recast the party as architects of a dynamic, fast-growing economy, it was not enough to simply cut deficits and lower interest rates. By explicitly identifying themselves with the financial sector, and with Wall Street in particular, the Democrats rebranded themselves as the party of an innovative, prosperous future. This historic rapprochement with the bankers—traditionally a Republican stronghold—began with an open door to financial-industry executives unprecedented for a Democratic White House.

Robert Rubin, the former co-chair of Goldman Sachs, was Clinton's first director of the National Economic Council and was promoted to Treasury secretary in 1995. Other Wall Street appointees included Gary Gensler of Goldman (Treasury undersecretary), Roger Altman of Lehman Brothers (deputy Treasury secretary), and Lee Sachs of Bear Stearns (assistant secretary for financial markets). Most surprisingly, in 1996 and again in 2000, Clinton reappointed Alan Greenspan—a libertarian free-market ideologue and onetime devotee of conservative intellectual darling Ayn Rand—as chair of the Federal Reserve Board of Governors.

More important, Clinton definitively reversed the Democratic Party's historic support for tight financial regulation. This dated back to the New Deal, when the Roosevelt administration and Congress had imposed sweeping constraints on the industry with the Glass-Steagall Act of 1933, the Securities Act of 1933, and the Securities Exchange Act of 1934. Financial deregulation had been one of the top priorities of President Reagan, but a decade later it was eagerly embraced by Democrats in both the White House and Congress. The Clinton years saw the Riegle-Neal Act of 1994, which opened the door to interstate banking and a wave of consolidation; the Gramm-Leach-Bliley Act of 1999, which dismantled the remaining barriers separating investment banking, commercial banking, and insurance; and the Commodity Futures Modernization Act of 2000, which effectively prohibited regulation of financial derivatives. All three bills were ultimately passed with major Democratic support in Congress. The Clinton administration even suppressed attempts by regulators to monitor excessive systemic risks—most famously when Rubin, Deputy Treasury Secretary Lawrence Summers, and Greenspan shut down a 1998 attempt by Brooksley Born, chair of the Commodity Futures Trading Commission, to study the possibility of increased oversight over derivatives.

The Democrats' new love affair with Wall Street was based on the theory that relaxing the rules governing financial institutions would stimulate innovation and promote the flow of capital to where it would do the most good for the economy. In particular, deregulation gave Democrats a shiny new housing story, free from the complications and negative connotations of public housing and Section 8 vouchers. Freeing markets for mortgages and mortgage-backed securities would increase the funding available to homebuyers, making it possible for more and more people to buy real estate—even if their incomes remained stagnant. As we know today, deregulation also made possible the highly concentrated and unstable financial system that collapsed in 2008, when the world suddenly realized that millions of those same mortgages could never be repaid.

At the time, however, catering to the financial industry dramatically increased the flow of campaign donations from Wall Street. Historically, banks and securities firms had leaned Republican, but the Clinton administration's embrace of deregulation—along with the Republican Party's increasingly hostile stances toward women, gays, and minorities—attracted more and more contributions precisely at the time when shrinking unions were unable to keep the party afloat. Bill Clinton, Barack Obama, and Hillary Clinton were all able to raise as much or more money from the financial sector than their Republican opponents for president.

The reconciliation between the Democratic Party and the financial industry also successfully redefined the party's economic identity. Prior to the 1990s, Democrats were associated with the old economy: heavy manufacturing, with its smokestacks, acid rain, and largely unionized workforces. But after the stagnation of the 1970s and the invasion by cheap Japanese cars, the American manufacturing industry was widely perceived to be in decline. By contrast, finance seemed a hotbed of innovation, beginning with the leveraged buyouts and junk bonds that marked the 1980s. Oliver Stone's 1987 movie *Wall Street* made corporate raider Gordon Gekko, best known for his "Greed is good" speech, a cultural icon; in 1989, Michael Lewis's memoir *Liar's Poker*, though written as an indictment of finance culture, helped make Wall Street the destination of choice for graduates of America's elite colleges. Finance was perceived to be clean, modern, and sophisticated—an industry that moved dollars instead of steel, that relied on brains instead of brawn.

Once upon a time, the Democratic Party helped the working class by supporting unions and promoting the social safety net. Now it claimed to help the working class by lubricating the flow of capital, which would promote economic growth and eventually create good jobs for everyone. Tired of being seen as for labor and against capital, the party could now be for everyone; or, in practice, it could be for capital while claiming to help labor as well. In less than a decade, the Democrats successfully repositioned themselves as the party of deficit reduction, welfare reform, market incentives, and financial innovation. The fact that the Clinton presidency coincided with a long economic expansion only sealed the bargain in Democrats' minds. From this point the party's platform would be technocratic management of a growing economy in which markets fulfill everyone's needs.

The 2000 presidential election demonstrated the weakness of this political strategy. Al Gore was the heir apparent, not only the two-term vice president, but also a fellow overeducated white Southerner and a longtime member of the Democratic Leadership Council. But when he tried to campaign on the continuation of the Clinton years (minus the sexual peccadilloes), it turned out that no one really knew what that meant. Without Clinton's personal charisma to close the deal, it wasn't clear that many voters wanted to buy the New Democrat brand—or that they could distinguish it from the empty "compassionate conservatism" that George W. Bush was peddling. In the late stages of the campaign, Gore tried to reinvent himself as a populist. "They're for the powerful. We're for the people," he declared, but by that point it was just an empty slogan.[26] Although overall economic growth had boosted the wages of lower-income workers, the administration he served in could point to few identifiable accomplishments that benefited "the people," and while the president himself had the political skill to square that circle, his lieutenant did not. And so the moderation of the Clinton years gave way to the disaster of the Bush years: two major tax cuts for the rich, an all-out campaign against economic regulation, and the most severe financial crisis and recession for 70 years.

The New Democrats, however, escaped the shipwreck of Gore's defeat with their prestige intact and only flourished during the next eight years. Indeed, they followed the model defined by conservative think tanks decades before, creating a network of Washington institutions that would house the "government in waiting" until the next shift in power. In addition to the Democratic Leadership Council, think tanks such as Third Way, the Progressive Policy Institute, the Center for American Progress, and the Hamilton Project (housed at the Brookings Institution) became refuges for Clinton administration alumni and sources of policy research favoring market-based solutions to economic problems. The Hamilton Project was founded by Robert Rubin, Clinton's Treasury secretary, and the Center for American Progress by John Podesta, Clinton's chief of staff. In Congress, Democrats used their new stature as responsible economic technocrats to criticize President Bush's tax cuts on the grounds that they threatened to increase budget deficits. For the most part, however, corruption, incompetence, and the Iraq War tarnished the Republican brand enough that Democrats could win an emphatic victory in 2006 without having to articulate a coherent economic agenda.

Hillary Clinton was the obvious first choice of the Democratic establishment for the 2008 presidential nomination, but Barack Obama fit the bill equally well—a smart, well-educated policy wonk who claimed to transcend party divisions. "There is not a liberal America and a conservative America—there is the United States of America," he proclaimed as a Senate candidate giving the keynote speech at the 2004

Democratic National Convention.[27] (After his election, Obama spoke at the launch of the Hamilton Project in 2006.)

Obama was arguably the most moderate of the main primary contenders; on health care, for example, he opposed the individual mandate proposed by Clinton (and later incorporated into Obamacare). He won the presidency largely on his personal story and charisma, an uplifting but vague promise of change, and general disaffection with Republicans that was exacerbated by the 2008 financial crisis. Obama's first inaugural address in 2009 was a masterpiece of triangulation, stereotyping and discarding both conservative and liberal positions in favor of an idealized center. "The question we ask today is not whether our government is too big or too small, but whether it works," the new president said. His economic philosophy was even more squarely in the Clinton tradition: "Nor is the question before us whether the market is a force for good or ill. Its power to generate wealth and expand freedom is unmatched. But this crisis has reminded us that without a watchful eye, the market can spin out of control."[28] In short, markets are the source of prosperity, and government's role is limited to ensuring that they function properly.

Barack Obama borrowed not only Bill Clinton's ideology, but also much of his staff. He turned over his transition team to Podesta, a longtime Clinton loyalist. Several of his Senate and campaign economic advisers were sidelined in favor of Clinton veterans. Among those taking top economic positions in the new administration were: Lawrence Summers, Robert Rubin's understudy and successor as Treasury secretary in the Clinton years; Timothy Geithner, an undersecretary to Summers and Rubin protégé; Peter Orszag, a former Clinton adviser and director of the Hamilton Project; Jason Furman, director of the Hamilton Project after Orszag; Michael Froman, Rubin's chief of staff in the Treasury Department; Gary Gensler, undersecretary for domestic finance under Summers; Mary Schapiro, head of the CFTC under Clinton; Neal Wolin, former general counsel of the Treasury Department; Jack Lew, former head of the Office of Management and Budget; and Michael Barr, a deputy assistant Treasury secretary under Rubin. When it came to economic affairs, it was clear that the new president was eager to embrace the legacy of the Clinton years.

Coming into office in the depths of the Great Recession, Obama's first task was to shore up a global financial system that had imploded the previous year and was only functioning thanks to oceans of liquidity provided by the Federal Reserve. At the same time, he had to rescue an economy that was shrinking rapidly and shedding jobs by the millions. Some members of the president's team considered nationalizing some of the sickest megabanks, particularly Citigroup and Bank of America, which clearly would have failed without government assistance (and whose recklessness had helped produce the financial crisis in the first place). But instead, the administration continued where its predecessor had left off, giving Citigroup a third bailout in February 2009 and effectively pledging unlimited support for the megabanks. Given the close relationships with the financial sector that had been fostered by the Clinton administration and maintained during the intervening years, the instinct of the Obama White House was to ride to the rescue of the banks they knew. Whereas Franklin Roosevelt positioned himself as an opponent of Wall Street, Obama styled himself as its protector. "My administration is the only thing between you and the pitchforks," he said to the CEOs of 13 large banks at the White House in March 2009.[29] As it turned out, that was a promise, not a threat, and Obama lived up to it, ensuring that the remaining large banks survived the crisis intact, with their CEOs in place.

The paralysis of the financial system was an unprecedented emergency, but the choice to rescue the megabanks that caused the crisis was a natural one for a Democratic establishment that prided itself on its sophisticated appreciation of modern finance. The Obama administration's broader response to the crisis and Great Recession demonstrated where the party now stood on key economic issues. The stimulus bill passed early in 2009 was far better than nothing, but it was constrained by the administration's dedication to fiscal responsibility, which the Clinton veterans saw as the keystone of both the 1990s boom and the Democrats' return to power. To preserve the party's deficit-fighting credentials, the stimulus had to be coupled with a "strategy to return to long-term fiscal discipline," in Furman's words.[30] Or, as Rahm Emanuel, Obama's first chief of staff, put it, "No fucking way is this number coming anywhere near a trillion dollars."[31] Therefore, the stimulus was too small to fill the hole created by the recession, while also designed to phase out quickly and avoid creating long-term government programs that could have had a lasting structural impact on the economy.

While the 2009 stimulus was merely inadequate, the administration's response to the housing crisis was unconscionable. The collapse of the housing bubble and the financial system inexorably produced wave after wave of delinquencies and foreclosures as homeowners, no longer able to refinance their houses, could not make their monthly payments. Yet the federal government never addressed the problems faced by ordinary families—once the backbone of the Democratic Party—with anything like the imagination or financial firepower it used to rescue the big banks. President Obama failed to follow through on his campaign proposal for mortgage "cramdown," which would have allowed bankruptcy judges to reduce the principal balance on mortgages. A plan by Treasury official Herb Allison to force banks to recognize losses on their bad loans was rejected by higher-ups because, in Allison's words, "We don't want to appear as though we're socialists."[32] (Allison was himself a seasoned capitalist, previously chief operating officer of Merrill Lynch and CEO of asset management giant TIAA.) The administration declined to pressure mortgage servicers to reduce the principal owed on mortgages, even in federally funded programs purportedly designed to help people stay in their homes. Any of these ideas would have hurt the banks' balance sheets, weakening them further.

Instead, the administration's main vehicle to help homeowners, the Home Affordable Modification Program, was designed as a voluntary program for mortgage servicers, promising them cash subsidies in exchange for reducing borrowers' monthly payments—another attempt to achieve public ends by giving a gentle nudge to private-sector institutions. The significant discretion handed to mortgage servicers enabled them to use the program as a predatory lending scheme, squeezing extra payments out of struggling borrowers before ultimately pursuing foreclosure. As Treasury Secretary Geithner infamously said, HAMP's real purpose was to "foam the runway for [banks]"—that is, to space out foreclosures long enough so that banks could absorb their losses without going under.[33] In other words, the administration's strategy was to let struggling families lose their homes in order to protect banks—an approach that clearly showed where their priorities lay. In the end, only a small fraction of delinquent homeowners received permanent loan modifications under HAMP, while more than nine million households lost their homes to foreclosure or financial distress.[34] In total, the Treasury Department only spent $29 billion on (mostly indirect) aid to homeowners, less than half of what the administration initially promised; to put this in context, families collectively lost more than $7 trillion in equity in their houses during the financial crisis.[35]

The disintegration of the banking system also demonstrated the need—and created the opportunity—for comprehensive reform of the financial sector. It was clear that decades of unchecked innovation, rampant deregulation, and excessive concentration had produced a financial system in which a handful of colossal banks preyed on unsophisticated borrowers while accumulating risks they scarcely understood, forcing the government to come to their rescue when they finally exploded. Unlike in 1933, however, the Obama administration and Democrats in

Congress chose not to pursue structural reform of the industry. Instead, the Dodd-Frank Act of 2010 re-engineered the regulatory framework of the financial sector, rearranging and in some cases increasing the powers available to government officials to oversee and potentially intervene in banks' operations.

The administration opposed proposals either to separate investment and commercial banking (by repealing the Gramm-Leach-Bliley Act) or to impose size limits on banks. After an amendment to establish size caps failed in the Senate, a senior Treasury official said, "If we'd been for it, it probably would have happened. But we weren't, so it didn't."[36] Lobbyists swarmed over Capitol Hill, picking off moderate Democrats—often longtime recipients of financial-industry support—to weaken the legislation even further. In 1933, Franklin Roosevelt had shut bankers out of his inner circle. By 2010, however, the Democratic Party was locked in a marriage with Wall Street, even if it was going through a rough patch at the time. A core tenet of the New Democrats was that finance is good and more finance is better, and one crisis was not enough to shake that belief. The result was a bill that largely preserved the financial system that was responsible for the 2008 crisis—and, indeed, America's largest banks today are even bigger than ever.

While financial reform was a battle that was thrust upon President Obama, he always intended health care to be the centerpiece of his legacy. The Patient Protection and Affordable Care Act of 2010 was the clearest demonstration yet of the Democratic Party's infatuation with market-based solutions to broad social problems. As late as the 1970s, party leaders had been proposing government-financed universal health insurance programs; even *Republican* Senator Jacob Javits introduced a Medicare for all bill in 1970. In 2010, by contrast, the party united behind a bill whose centerpiece was exchanges, in which insurers would supposedly compete for consumers by providing better health plans at lower prices.

The administration's experts knew that health insurance markets, left on their own, would produce unwanted outcomes. Poor people simply wouldn't be able to afford coverage; people might be tricked into buying deceptive policies that turned out to provide minimal benefits when they were actually needed; and, because of adverse selection, insurers would set high prices that only sick people would be willing to pay (if they could afford them). To address these problems, the Affordable Care Act included subsidies for lower-income families, minimum coverage requirements, and the individual mandate, which was designed to force healthy people to buy insurance, bringing down prices for everyone.

Obamacare, as it came to be known, was an improvement on the unregulated individual market that preceded it. But as an exercise in Democratic policymaking, it was remarkable for its insistence on using markets and the private sector to achieve public ends—which, in this case, could be much more simply accomplished with a traditional social insurance program such as Social Security or Medicare. The root problem with the American health care system is that care is expensive; the average total premium for an employer-sponsored family plan is more than $20,000 even before deductibles and co-payments, far more than many workers could afford.[37] In a properly functioning market, people who can't afford something don't get it. But when it comes to health care, that's not an outcome we are willing to accept. No one will say (in public, at least) that how much you suffer, or whether you live or die, should depend on how much money you have—although in practice that's often how it works. Instead, Republicans and Democrats agree that all people should have access to decent health care at a price they can afford.

The most direct way to realize this goal is a universal health insurance plan (often known as "single payer") paid for by a progressive tax system; that way everyone has coverage, and the amount you pay depends on your income. But the core assumption behind the Affordable Care Act was that competitive markets are the best way to provide goods and services, and the role of government is limited to ensuring that markets function properly. That's why we ended up with a complicated system designed to contort markets into producing socially acceptable outcomes, whose features include private insurers whose costs are significantly *higher* than Medicare's; complicated risk adjustment mechanisms designed to ensure that insurers aren't profiting by skimming off the healthiest customers; subsidies that aren't enough for many families; coverage for the poor that is subject to the whims of state governors and legislatures; annual negotiations in which insurers threaten to pull out of the exchanges unless they can raise prices; and, because underlying health care costs continue to rise, plans that increasingly require more out-of-pocket spending by customers.

Despite all the attention paid to the private health insurance exchanges, it is telling that the part of the Affordable Care Act that expanded coverage the most was actually an expansion of *public* insurance: the increase in Medicaid eligibility up to 138 percent of the federal poverty level. This one provision alone gave health insurance to 14 million Americans, far more than the increase in coverage in the individual market—even though many Republican governors and legislatures chose not to adopt the Medicaid expansion.[38]

Defenders of Obamacare point out that there were not enough votes for a universal single-payer system. But there is no evidence that the architects of the Affordable Care Act would have preferred single-payer; instead, they seem to have been firmly in favor of private markets. More to the point, the question of votes only deflects the question. Exactly zero Republicans voted for the final version of the Affordable Care Act. The health care reform we got was the health care reform that the Democratic Party wanted—whether for ideological reasons, or because its members wanted to stay on good terms with the insurance industry. The Democratic position was once that we should pool our resources to ensure that everyone is protected against certain shared risks, including lack of access to health care. Now the default approach was to assume that markets can provide all good things and then, if necessary, figure out how to make those markets work better. Obamacare fit perfectly with the new worldview of Democratic insiders, who rejected anything that might be seen as socialist and portrayed themselves as sophisticated, business-friendly architects of enlightened policies informed by the latest economic research.

Although finance and health care dominated President Obama's legislative agenda, other components of his economic agenda betrayed the same preference for technocratic, market-based solutions. Retirement security has been a ticking time bomb for decades, made worse by the collapse of home values beginning in 2006. The traditional Democratic approach to retirement was Social Security—a mandatory, government-run program that provides minimum benefits to virtually every worker. Obama's answer, however, was a proposal to require companies to automatically enroll their employees into 401(k) individual saving plans administered by the private asset management industry. This was a classic New Democrat proposal, giving private markets a nudge to help them achieve public ends—in this case, a nudge based on the hot new field of behavioral economics. It also fit the New Democrat mold by failing to address the root cause of retirement insecurity: After decades of wage stagnation, many people just don't make enough money to save. Unwilling to propose anything that smacked of redistribution, Obama was left talking about the power of the stock market to multiply wealth—scant consolation to workers who have none to begin with.

As for Social Security, President Obama was willing to offer a major long-term reduction in benefits (by changing the way cost-of-living adjustments are calculated) in his pursuit of a budgetary deal with Republicans. When negotiations failed, he even included the same benefit reduction in his 2014 budget proposal as a way to reduce long-term deficits—since the Clinton administration, Democrats' way of showing their tough-mindedness on economic issues.

President Obama also inherited Clinton's market-oriented approach to education. His administration took up the buzzword of "accountability," backing the development of the Common Core standards and providing incentives to states to develop teacher evaluation systems based on standardized test scores. The Race to the Top program dangled money to states strapped for cash after the recession, rewarding those that attempted to expand the market share of charter schools. Obama went one further than Clinton in the student loan market, completely eliminating federal subsidies to private banks. In addition, the administration created a new loan repayment plan that links payments to the borrower's income, while requiring universities to demonstrate that their graduates were actually able to get jobs, and issuing a rule helping people who had been defrauded by for-profit institutions. These were welcome changes. But after a generation of rapidly rising tuition costs, and with outstanding loans doubling to $1.4 trillion during the president's tenure,[39] they barely made a dent in the ballooning student debt crisis. Making it a little easier to borrow money was no solution to the fundamental problem: that college costs were rising much faster than incomes.

With time running out on his second term, President Obama pinned his hopes for one more economic policy victory on the Trans-Pacific Partnership, a trade agreement negotiated between a dozen countries bordering the Pacific Ocean. For the administration, the TPP was simply a matter of basic economics: International trade contributes to economic growth, creating jobs in export industries and lowering prices for consumers. Opponents of the agreement, Obama's team insisted, were simply old-fashioned protectionists who didn't understand the magic of markets.

Even in the economics textbook, however, trade creates winners and losers, and since the invasion of our markets by Chinese exports, the United States has not done a good job of protecting the losers—primarily people dependent on industries threatened by foreign competition. In addition, TPP was far more than a free-trade agreement. Among other things, its intellectual-property rules forced other countries to adopt laws protecting the (U.S.-dominated) media and pharmaceutical industries, and its system for "investor-state dispute settlement" allowed multinational corporations to bypass domestic legal systems—fostering the belief that TPP was primarily drafted to benefit big business. Politically, TPP ultimately became a casualty of the populist rebellion of 2016, leaving a Democratic president as the last supporter of a trade agreement rejected by both the left and the right—an outcome that would have seemed fantastic only 30 years before.

To be sure, there are other voices in the Democratic Party, which has not been entirely taken over by pro-business, pro-market ideas and policies. Presidents Clinton and Obama, however, almost by definition constitute the center of gravity of the party. Their ideas, their legacy, and their people make up the current Democratic establishment. In addition, in an age of short memory spans, they represent what the party means to most Americans today; its identity is largely a creation of their words and their actions. Hillary Clinton certainly did little to reposition the Democratic Party in the eyes of most people. Her economic platform was a caricature of New Democrat technocracy, with its catalog of bulleted plans, its painstaking care to distinguish itself from opponents on both the right and the left, the overbearing sophistication with which it lectured that Bernie Sanders's proposals were impractical, and its lack of any message beyond a promise to create economic growth and good jobs. Clinton's few, faltering endorsements of progressive positions—such as her switch from supporting to opposing the TPP—only came after considerable pressure from the left, and only reinforced the idea that the Democratic standard-bearer stood for nothing more than grinding out every last vote possible in the upcoming election.

This brings us to the Democratic Party of today. Leaving aside the recent progressive insurrection—inspired by Sanders and embodied by Alexandria Ocasio-Cortez and the Squad—it is a party devoid of any compelling idea of how to address the fundamental economic challenges our country faces today: wage stagnation, the rising cost of health care and urban housing, the precariousness of most jobs, and extreme inequality. After defining themselves in opposition to old-fashioned government spending programs that smacked suspiciously of redistribution, after embracing the doctrine of market-based solutions, and after insisting for decades that economic growth would solve all problems, establishment Democrats today have nothing left to offer.

Their economic policy agenda is anemic, constrained as it is by the premise that all good things must come from the market. Infrastructure spending is a perennial favorite, because it addresses a market failure (private companies have insufficient incentive to build or maintain shared goods like roads and bridges), can be touted as a productive long-term investment, and can be channeled through the private sector. Job retraining programs are another staple, because they promise to help workers adapt to changes in the labor market—a promise that, unfortunately, they often fail to keep.

Otherwise, there is precious little. The idea of a $15 minimum wage was the product of progressive groups on the state and local levels, only later reluctantly embraced by party leaders. Medicare for All likewise was born on the party's left wing, and the establishment currently appears to be trying to figure out how best to squash the idea without being blamed for doing so. The idea that the government should increase taxes on the rich and *give* stuff to ordinary people (a college education, for example) is anathema, condemned as class warfare by moderate Democrats even more vigorously than by Republicans.

This is the economic vision of their Democratic Party. Economic growth is the goal, markets are the means, and the role of government is to maximize efficiency by correcting for specific market failures. The things people actually want—such as education, jobs, housing, and health care—are a by-product of that growth. Heavy-handed attempts to intervene in the economy will only backfire.

The fact that we would have called this a moderate Republican vision only a few years ago doesn't necessarily make it wrong. And it isn't nonsensical on its face. The problem is that it has failed, both as policy and as politics.

CHAPTER 2

Bad Policy

There are only two families in the world, my old grandmother used to say, the Haves and the Have-nots.
  —Sancho, in *Don Quixote*[40]

Things have not changed so much since the days when Miguel de Cervantes wrote *Don Quixote*. There are exceptionally wealthy families, and then there is everyone else. As a society, we clearly have the capacity to produce enough goods and services to enable everyone to live in material comfort, with decent food and clothing, a safe place to live, a comprehensive education from preschool through college, and even a reasonable amount of health care. The total income of all Americans is more than $54,000 per person—that's more than $210,000 for a family of four.[41] Yet many people can barely get by. Even in what we often call the richest country in human history, almost 40 million people live in households that struggle to obtain enough food.[42]

Inequality and economic hardship have long been characteristics of human civilization, at least since the advent of agriculture more than ten thousand years ago. At first glance, it might seem that wealthy people, who need money the least, should share some of their riches with everyone else. In fact, both Social Security and Medicare—the most popular federal government programs in existence—rely on a modest degree of redistribution. But this is not how the American political system works today. Instead, Republicans and most Democrats agree that competitive markets and economic growth are the best way to help both the 99 percent and the 1 percent—that "a rising tide lifts all boats" (a saying commonly attributed to President John F. Kennedy). As long as the total pie is getting bigger, the logic goes, each person will get a larger slice; therefore, what we should care about is overall economic growth.

This principle was the basis for the accommodation between labor and capital in the Western bloc after World War II. Workers' parties abandoned the ideas of violent revolution and state control of the means of production, settling instead for workers' rights, nationalization of a few key industries (in some European countries), and a generous welfare state. For the business sector, a robust social safety net was a fair price to pay for political stability and the preservation of capitalism. Instead of the government organizing production and then sharing everything more or less equally ("To each according to his needs," in the words of Karl Marx), the private sector would be modestly regulated, people would make what they could earn in the market, and then tax-funded government programs would make sure no one was completely destitute. Even with a large degree of inequality, economic growth would make all social classes continually better off over time. The assembly-line worker in the automobile factory would earn only a fraction of what the company CEO took home, but his standard of living would rise over his lifetime, and he knew that the inexorable march of prosperity promised a better future for his children.

The rising tide was the theoretical basis for the "trickle-down economics" of President Ronald Reagan and the conservative revolution. In their view, the postwar American economy already suffered from too much redistribution; cutting taxes for the rich would encourage them to work, save, and invest, accelerating growth and therefore benefiting all people. But it was also the justification for the opposition's New Democrat narrative of growth and opportunity. "This isn't the time to get caught up in distributional politics," Democratic Leadership Council Chair Charles Robb said in 1986—"it's time to make the economic pie grow."[43]

Bill Clinton agreed. "The Democratic Party's fundamental mission," he wrote, is "to expand opportunity, not government; to recognize that economic growth is a prerequisite for expanding opportunity; to invest in the skills and ingenuity of our people in order to build shared prosperity."[44] In short, the key to making everyone better off is to encourage private-sector growth, while "expanding opportunity" to ensure that no one is left behind. Clinton's primary domestic policy achievements included lower deficits, welfare reform, and financial deregulation, all traditional Republican goals; yet as long as economic growth was good for rich and poor alike, he could still claim that he was a champion of ordinary men and women.

The fundamental economic fact of our lifetimes is that this premise no longer holds. Growth no longer benefits all strata of society. Instead, the overwhelming majority of the gains from material progress are being claimed by people who are already very rich, while everyone else is left to share the crumbs.

To see what has gone wrong with the American economy, it's first important to understand what growth is and why it makes people better off. We say an economy grows when the total amount of goods and services it produces—often called gross domestic product, or GDP—increases from year to year. A country's GDP is mainly determined by the number of people in the economy (population) and the average amount that each person can produce (productivity). Over the long term, growth in GDP usually results either from an increase in population or from an increase in productivity. The former, however, makes people no better off on average because more stuff has to be divided among more people. It is only productivity growth that leads to higher standards of living. When we get better at making things, we end up with more things per person.

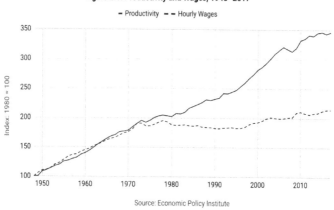

Figure 2.1: Productivity and Wages, 1948–2017

Source: Economic Policy Institute

In other words, a rising standard of living is only made possible by long-term increases in productivity. Fortunately for us, productivity has been climbing higher since the beginning of the Industrial Revolution, and in particular since World War II. From 1948 until 1972, as shown in Figure 2.1,[45] productivity rose at an average rate of 2.7 percent per year, and wages grew at exactly the same rate (after adjusting for inflation). As people got better at making stuff, they were paid more to make it. This makes intuitive sense, because if a worker can produce twice as much as before, her labor is worth twice as much to her company. When this is the case, economic growth does make most people better off, because ordinary workers are getting a fair share of its benefits.

Since 1972, however, the story has completely changed. Productivity has continued to grow, albeit more slowly (at an average annual rate of 1.3 percent). But in contrast to previous decades, workers have received only a small fraction of those gains in the form of higher wages, which have increased at a rate of less than 0.3 percent per year. People got better at making stuff, and therefore the economy got bigger—but most of them did not get a fair share of that growth. On average, a worker in 2017 could produce 82 percent more per hour than a worker in 1972, but was only paid 13 percent more.

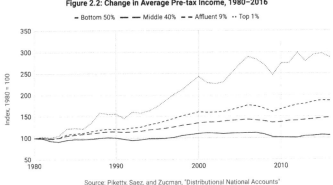

Figure 2.2: Change in Average Pre-tax Income, 1980–2016

Source: Piketty, Saez, and Zucman, "Distributional National Accounts"

So where instead did the benefits of higher productivity and economic growth go? The answer is simple: to the very rich.

Figure 2.2[46] shows how market forces have distributed the benefits of growth across different social strata between 1980 and 2016. (Figures 2.2 and 2.3 are from research by Thomas Piketty, Emmanuel Saez, and Gabriel Zucman, probably the most prominent economists studying income and wealth inequality today. Their latest series end in 2016; all figures are adjusted for inflation.) Incomes for the bottom 50 percent of the population (solid line) have barely budged. In other words, half of our country gained virtually no material benefit from 36 years of economic growth. In the meantime, the incomes of the top 1 percent (top dotted line) have tripled; the groups in between have done modestly better than the bottom 50 percent, but have not enjoyed anything like the rewards flowing to the very rich. (People in the top 0.1 percent did even better; their incomes almost quadrupled.) It is by now well known that the 1 percent have gained a much larger *share* of national income in

Figure 2.3: Change in Average Pre-tax Income for Bottom 50% by Age Group, 1980–2016

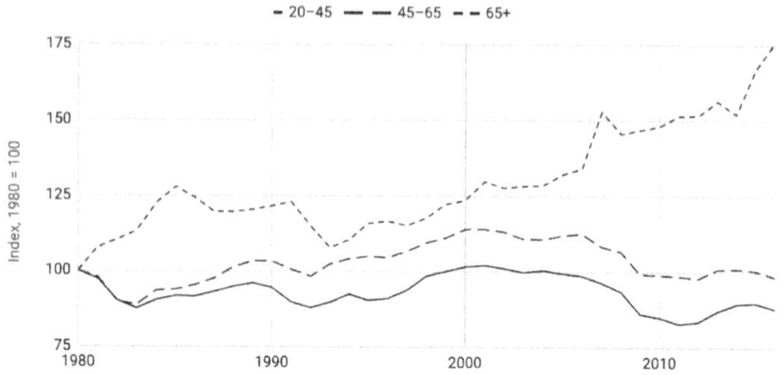

Source: Piketty, Saez, and Zucman, "Distributional National Accounts"

recent decades; in the process, as this figure shows, they have left almost nothing for much of the population.

But things are actually worse than they seem. Figure 2.3[47] shows the change in average income since 1980 for people in the bottom 50 percent of the distribution—that is, the half of the country that was once associated with the Democratic Party. Within this group, working-age adults, particularly younger ones (solid line), are making less than they did in 1980; only the elderly (top dashed line) are better off, because of rising Social Security and pension payouts. If we look instead at after-tax income—taking into account taxes and government spending—the picture is only slightly improved. Average after-tax income for the poorer half of the population increased by 25 percent (about 0.8 percent per year), but all of this growth was enjoyed by the elderly, thanks in large part to the rising dollar value of Medicare.[48]

There are many reasons why the wealthy have been the primary beneficiaries of increased productivity in recent decades. The most important explanation is a shift in the balance of power between labor and capital. If companies can make 82 percent more stuff while only paying workers 13 percent more, their per-unit costs are lower. Lower costs result in some combination of lower prices, which help everyone, and higher profits, which benefit the owners of those businesses. Those owners are largely rich people, virtually by definition; their equity holdings in companies, either directly or through stock portfolios, is what makes them rich. And lower prices on many consumer goods have been more than canceled out by severe increases in the cost of health care, education, and housing.

A second obvious reason why the rich have done so much better than everyone else has been tax cuts that favor the wealthy—particularly tax cuts on capital income. These were primarily the work of Republicans, including the 1981 Reagan tax cut and the 2001 and 2003 Bush tax cuts, but Democrats had a part to play as well—the Clinton administration with the 1997 capital gains tax cut, and the Obama administration with the 2013 deal that made permanent most of the Bush tax cuts. Other factors include globalization and technology, which have enabled highly educated, highly skilled people to earn more money by serving larger markets more efficiently than before.

Growth has not been widely shared in the contemporary U.S. economy—and neither has opportunity, the other pillar of the New Democrat ideology. The economic importance of a college education has never been greater, yet children from affluent families are more than four times as likely to earn a bachelor's degree as children from poor families. Large gaps in educational outcomes exist even between students with similar levels of academic preparation, as indicated by standardized assessments.[49] More disturbing still, when comparing people born in the 1980s to those born in the 1970s, the advantages of wealth have only grown. Even as more children of lower-income families have attended college (in part thanks to the greater availability of student loans), their chances of earning a degree have actually declined; by contrast, rich children have become much more likely to successfully graduate.[50]

In short, since the 1970s, the tide has continued to rise, but it has not lifted all boats—only the luxury yachts of the super-rich. In the 1970s, 1 percent of the population owned 20–25 percent of total wealth; today they own about 40 percent of everything that can be traced—and considerably more if you include the likely assets hidden in offshore tax havens.[51] The economy does a decent job of increasing productivity and therefore generating growth in total output, but leaves ordinary people little better off than they were 40 years ago. For example, the typical man working a full-time, year-round job earned $51,640 in 2016—after adjusting for inflation, only *$16* more than in 1976.[52] Overall, median household income in 2017 was only 19 percent higher than in 1973[53]—an increase of less than 0.5 percent per year—and has been essentially flat since 1999.[54] The Great Recession wiped out all wealth gains for the bottom 50 percent of the population since the 1950s; by 2016, this group was only as rich as it had been in the late 1960s.[55]

Looking at the most intuitive measure of the so-called American dream, there is no longer any reason to be confident that children will do better than their parents. The rate of absolute mobility—making more money than one's parents—was more than 90 percent for people born in 1940, but only 50 percent for those born in 1980. And growth alone cannot be the answer; given the way economic rewards are distributed today, we would need annual growth rates exceeding 6 percent—a virtual impossibility—to restore the levels of absolute mobility enjoyed by people born in the 1940s.[56]

With Democrats in the White House for 16 of the past 27 years, we cannot simply blame this situation on the Republicans. Since the Clinton administration, the overarching economic strategy of the Democratic establishment has been to foster overall economic growth rather than aiding struggling families directly, on the premise that everyone would benefit in the long run. But even to the extent those policies helped the economy expand—for example, low deficits in the 1990s may have contributed to that decade's boom—it is clear in retrospect that they only had the effect of making a thin stratum of rich people even richer. In addition, many of the signature policies of the Clinton and Obama administrations turned out to be directly harmful to poor and working-class people.

Welfare reform was the core domestic policy achievement of the Clinton presidency. Tightened eligibility requirements for cash assistance and lifetime benefit caps did have the intended result of reducing the number of people on welfare, which fell by more than half. But contrary to the facile predictions of the bill's supporters, people who lost government benefit checks did not magically become productive workers able to support themselves. Those with superior skills or educational attainment were able to find decent jobs, especially in the booming economy of the late 1990s, and many also benefited from contemporaneous increases in the Earned Income Tax Credit. But another group of people left welfare for low-wage jobs that barely made up for the cash assistance they had lost, while many others—about 40 percent of former recipients—were unable to find jobs and were forced to struggle without either paying jobs or cash assistance.[57] The number of people in deep poverty—those in households receiving less than half of the poverty threshold—increased after the 1996 bill, largely because of its restrictions on cash assistance.[58]

The Personal Responsibility and Work Opportunity Reconciliation Act of 1996 made life much harder for the most vulnerable populations—people without the education, skills, or stable health necessary to find and keep steady jobs. In addition to imposing a five-year cap on cash assistance, the bill gave states the ability to impose harsher restrictions. The Arizona legislature, for example, recently set a one-year limit on welfare benefits—which were already only $278 per month for a family of three.[59] Across the country, the result has been a sharp rise in families that have virtually no cash income—less than $2 per person, per day. The number of children living in these extremely poor households almost tripled from 415,000 in 1995 to 1.2 million in 2012 (even after adjusting for underreporting of income);[60] the increase was even more rapid in single-mother households. Poor people who used to be able to rely on a small check from the government now must resort to blood donations (which have almost tripled since the late 1990s[61]), food pantries (whose clients have more than doubled[62]), collecting recyclable containers, and selling food stamps at a deep discount.

As welfare reform consigned some poor families to destitution and economic hopelessness, it also left both federal and state governments free to ignore their plight. Out of every dollar spent under the Temporary Assistance for Needy Families (TANF) umbrella, only 26 cents provide cash assistance to poor families, and another 24 cents fund programs to help poor people get and keep jobs. The other 50 cents (or much more in some states) is diverted to other uses ranging from educational scholarships to the child welfare system to marriage counseling (with a full 8 cents dedicated to "preventing out-of-wedlock pregnancies").[63] The consequence is that only 23 percent of families in poverty actually get any financial support from TANF.[64] The meagerness of our welfare system was particularly apparent during the Great Recession, when the number of families receiving assistance barely budged even as the unemployment rate more than doubled—not a surprising outcome, given that TANF is funded as a block grant that grows more slowly than inflation.[65] Turning to market incentives to address the challenge of poverty had exactly the outcome we should have expected: Those people better able to sell their skills in the market economy became better off, while those without the ability to compete—often through no fault of their own—suffered.

The flaws of welfare reform have gone largely unnoticed because few people pay much attention to the plight of the poor. By contrast, the Democratic Party's embrace of financial deregulation turned out to be a spectacular catastrophe. Clinton-era financial policy rested on two basic premises: First, relaxing constraints on the banking and securities markets would unleash innovation, expanding access to capital and turbocharging the economy; and second, market forces and the self-interest of sophisticated institutions would protect consumers from abuse and ensure the safety of the overall system. These assumptions were calamitously wrong.

Deregulation had exactly the immediate results that its supporters predicted. There was a huge increase in concentration in the financial sector, as banks combined with each other in mergers of ever-increasing scale and scope. To take just one example, NationsBank bought Boatmen's Bancshares in 1996 and Barnett Bank in 1997, becoming the biggest bank in the country; in 1998, NationsBank merged with Bank of America (which had absorbed Security Pacific in 1992); and in 2004, the new Bank of America bought FleetBoston (itself the merger of the three largest banks in New England).

At the same time, the Gramm-Leach-Bliley Act of 1999, along with earlier rulings by the Federal Reserve, made possible a new generation of mega-institutions that did everything from taking deposits and making commercial loans to structuring and underwriting complex securities, trading customized derivatives, and placing massive proprietary bets on the direction of markets. In virtually every case, the risk-loving culture of the investment banks (where people talked about "ripping the face off" their customers) dominated the once more conservative outlook of the commercial bankers. And deregulation certainly fostered financial innovation. Of the many brilliant ideas churned out by the wizards of Wall Street, the most important was the structured asset-backed security, epitomized by the mortgage-backed security (MBS) and collateralized debt obligation (CDO). These new creations allowed banks to pool together a large number of mortgages and repackage them as multiple flavors of MBSs with customized risk and return characteristics—and then repeat the process, using those MBSs as inputs to create CDOs. By selling these MBSs, CDOs, and even third-generation CDO-squared products to investors, the banks vastly increased the amount of money available for the housing market, spurring a rapid escalation in home construction.

This influx of capital did lower interest rates for homeowners. But the steady stream of profits from structured securities spurred demand for loans, particularly the subprime mortgages that made the best raw material for MBSs. A rapidly growing industry of mortgage lenders and brokers targeted millions of largely unsuspecting borrowers, pushing toxic products such as the option adjustable rate mortgage, whose monthly payments could explode upward after a teaser period of two or three years. Lenders falsified loan applications or simply agreed not to verify borrowers' income; the investment banks packaging mortgages together overlooked evidence of fraud or shoddy underwriting, eager to get their hands on higher-cost loans that could yield more in the secondary market.

The result of this frenzy of lending and securitization was the largest housing bubble in modern history. Even after it peaked in 2006, the large banks continued squeezing profits out of a housing industry they knew was heading for a crash, selling synthetic CDOs based not on actual MBSs, but on side bets for and against existing securities. When the bubble finally imploded in 2008, many securities that were supposed to be utterly safe turned out to be worthless. The megabanks that a generation of policymakers had hailed as the engine of capitalism were worthless as well, their balance sheets weighed down by toxic assets they had concocted themselves. Hundreds of acres of unfinished developments were left to rot in the sun in Florida and the Southwest, and the shock waves of a collapsing financial system paralyzed the real economy, producing the worst downturn since the Great Depression. Most galling, the banks that had for decades been lobbying to be left alone by Washington came begging for federal support. Both the Bush and Obama administrations obliged, bailing them out on generous terms, rescuing both their CEOs and their shareholders from their mistakes.

The bottom line of the financial crisis is virtually incalculable: nine million families forced out of their homes, almost nine million jobs lost, record levels of long-term unemployment, trillions of dollars in lost output, and an economy whose overall capacity has been damaged for the foreseeable future. But those losses were not spread evenly. Although rich people lost paper wealth when the stock market plummeted at the height of the crisis, by 2019 the S&P 500 index had more than quadrupled from its lows—and almost doubled since its earlier peak in 2007. The median family in the top 10 percent of the income distribution was 27 percent richer in 2016 than before the crash, and is worth considerably more today.[66] Wall Street bonuses rebounded to their pre-crisis levels, reaching $184,000 on average by 2017.[67] Highly skilled, well-paid people living in winner-take-all cities, such as San Francisco, New York, Washington, and Boston, have thrived as the economy continues to grow.

On the other hand … Employees with mid-level skills were replaced by more educated workers or by machines. Rural communities hemorrhaged businesses and jobs that will probably never return. People who lost their homes to foreclosure, their credit records ruined, were unable to benefit from the housing recovery. Because minority borrowers were more likely to have taken out high-cost mortgages, the financial crisis and Great Recession exacerbated differences in wealth across racial and ethnic groups.[68] The percentage of households owning their own homes fell to its lowest point in 50 years; even after a modest recovery, home-ownership rates for all groups except the elderly are lower than in the 1980s.[69] Long-neglected government programs for public or subsidized rental housing have been overrun by the need for affordable rentals in expensive cities; the proportion of eligible families receiving any housing assistance has fallen to 25 percent.[70] In 2016, the median family had a net worth 29 percent lower than in 2007.[71] In the long run, financial deregulation only deepened the growing divide between the haves and the have-nots in America.

The verdict on Democratic health care reform is not quite so bleak. The Affordable Care Act undoubtedly helped many poor and middle-class families, particularly by expanding eligibility for Medicaid (at least in states whose Republican governments did not reject federal money out of spite) and by helping people without employer-sponsored coverage buy health insurance. But the cracks in Obamacare were already visible before the Trump administration set out to undermine it, for the simple reason that the program could never be a solution to our fundamental health care problem: Modern medicine in the United States is expensive. In aggregate, we spend more than $10,000 per person on health care—almost twice as much as in other rich countries[72]—and the sector continues to grow faster than the economy as a whole.[73] Obamacare makes it easier for people to shop for health plans, but it relies on private, profit-seeking insurers, so we have to let them pass rising prices through to all of us—or they will simply pull out of the market. (The Affordable Care Act eliminated insurers' other option, which was to stop covering sick people.) Even after a slight dip in 2019, benchmark premiums for policies sold on the new health insurance exchanges have grown at an average annual rate of 12 percent since they were introduced for the 2014 coverage year.[74] Premiums in the employer-sponsored market have also increased faster than inflation; in 2019, the average family plan costs $20,576, of which the employee pays $6,015 directly.[75]

Premiums tell only part of the story. We are also living through a major change in what it means to have health insurance in the first place. More and more policies today demand high levels of cost sharing, also known as out-of-pocket payments, in the form of deductibles, co-payments, and coinsurance. There are two reasons for this shift. One is the idea that, for markets to function properly, consumers have to have the right incentives; forcing people to pay a significant share of their health care costs will make them buy less. The second reason is that insurers can offer lower up-front premiums by shifting the real cost of insurance to the time of service; families on a tight budget may only be able to afford plans with low premiums now that will require high out-of-pocket payments later.

Both of these factors have contributed to the rise of the high-deductible health plan (HDHP), which requires people to pay a large deductible before their coverage kicks in—in other words, health insurance that many people cannot afford to use. These policies essentially did not exist before the George W. Bush administration; by 2018, 30 percent of workers with employer-sponsored insurance were enrolled in HDHPs, with an average deductible for family coverage well over $4,000.[76] As for Obamacare, the vast majority of the plans that people buy on the exchanges have high deductibles.[77]

This is why the headline problem with our health care system is no longer that people don't have coverage at all (although the proportion of people who are uninsured has crept back up to 13.7 percent in recent years[78]), but that too many nominally insured people can't afford the care they need. For example, even after subsidies, a family of four earning $60,000 would have to pay $4,608 per year for a "silver" plan, and then could have to pay up to $13,000 in deductibles and co-payments.[79] That's a lot of money. And it doesn't even include charges for out-of-network services, which usually are not covered by Obamacare plans. (One way that insurers control prices is by negotiating preferred rates with a narrow network of doctors and hospitals, but then refusing to cover services by other providers.)

Since the Affordable Care Act was passed in 2010, the decrease in the uninsured has been almost perfectly balanced by an increase in the underinsured—people whose premiums or out-of-pocket spending place a heavy burden on their finances. As of 2018, 37 percent of adults reported trouble paying medical bills, and 35 percent said they declined needed care because of costs.[80] Of working- and middle-class adults (those making less than 2.5 times the poverty line), half are not confident that they could afford to pay for a serious illness, and two-thirds would be unable to pay an unexpected $1,000 medical bill.[81] At the end of the day, insurers have responded to rising healthcare costs simply by providing less coverage for more money.

Unfortunately, there is reason to think things will only get worse. As long as the cost of medical care continues to increase, we either need to get less of it or pay more. If we insist on keeping premiums "affordable," then the price of insurance—whether employer group plans or individual policies bought on exchanges—has to be shifted to out-of-pocket payments. People who can't afford those payments, or who couldn't afford the premiums in the first place, will have to go without needed care. Obamacare was a heroic effort to solve the problem of the uninsured, and it made things better in the short term. But any system based on competition between private insurers will lack the market power to rein in an out-of-control health care industry. In the meantime, the overall landscape is becoming more and more unequal: People with steady jobs at large employers have the best plans, while those working for small businesses and the casually employed are more likely to be stuck with policies that turn out to be inadequate when emergency strikes.

In short, the signature economic policies of the past two Democratic presidents have done little to help, and have in some cases harmed, the working- and middle-class families that their party once represented. Welfare reform, financial deregulation, and Obamacare were technocratic, market-oriented programs backed up by reams of white papers mass-produced by think tanks and government agencies. They were popular with the Democratic policy elite because they promised to benefit everyone without offending the corporate sector's desire for profits, in contrast to an imagined past of naked redistribution from rich to poor. Their legacy, however, was an increase in extreme poverty, a ruinous financial crisis and recession, and a health care system destined to collapse under the weight of mounting costs.

More important still is what the most recent Democratic regimes did not do. Confident that a rising tide would lift all boats, they did little to confront rising inequality, even as President Obama—who could certainly talk a good game—called it the "defining challenge of our time."[82] Inequality has many causes, ranging from globalization and technology to school resegregation and changes in the tax code. But the economic platform introduced by the New Democrats, with its market-based solutions and its focus on overall growth (rather than who benefits from that growth), provided a convenient excuse to do nothing about inequality itself, nothing to help the people getting left behind with the wrong job skills or in the wrong part of the country. Both Presidents Clinton and Obama pointed with pride to the long economic booms during their tenures—overlooking the fact that it was precisely during those times that the very rich opened up the tremendous gap that separates them from everyone else.

Too much of what passes for Democratic economic policy still suffers the same basic flaw: wanting to believe that some clever, market-oriented, unmistakably capitalist policy idea will help low- and middle-income families. In recent years, the two main proposals that most Democrats could agree on have been infrastructure spending and investment in clean technology. Both of these are undeniably good ideas. Better infrastructure, both physical and digital, should promote innovation and economic activity. Research, development, and commercialization of renewable-energy technologies are urgently needed if we are to limit the impact of climate change to any kind of tolerable level. But these proposals are too small and too poorly targeted to do much to address wage stagnation and inequality. Most infrastructure spending plans would simply provide a short-term boost to the construction sector and otherwise leave intact the economic forces that allow the rich to appropriate the benefits of economic growth. Clean-technology investment would flow through the same venture capital network that turns select members of the educational elite into billionaires while providing enviable returns to well-connected institutional investors. There is no reason to believe that either of these ideas would change the fundamental dynamic of the past four decades: When good things happen to the economy, it is the wealthy few who benefit.

The crucial problem we must face is how the gains from economic progress are divided. Ideas that would actually address that problem arise only on the left of the Democratic Party, and then are usually resisted stubbornly (though often quietly, behind the scenes) by the establishment. A few manage to break through by sheer force of popularity, such as the campaign for a $15 minimum wage, but they are the exception. Even Medicare for All—which has majority support among the entire population, let alone Democrats[83]—faces bitter resistance from centrists still terrified of being tagged as tax-and-spend liberals, hiding behind the Clintonite cloak of fiscal responsibility.

Growing awareness of inequality has prompted a new wave of thinking about how to affect the "predistribution" of income—that is, how the benefits of economic activity are divided before government intervention via taxes and spending programs. The minimum wage can be thought of as a policy tool aimed at predistribution, because it generally increases employees' wages at the expense of company owners and customers. Rules that make it easier for unions to organize similarly enable workers to take home a larger share of the surplus that they create. Breaking up or aggressively regulating the large companies that dominate many sectors of our economy would begin to reverse the harms caused by decades of increasing market concentration, including lower wages for employees, higher prices for customers, and reduced innovation. Thinking about the distributional outcomes produced by our economic system is undeniably better than focusing solely on overall growth.

At the same time, however, improving the way the market allocates income between the shop floor, the executive suite, and the owner's mansion will not be enough to undo the damage done by decades of bipartisan market boosterism. We enter the economic arena with vastly unequal endowments of wealth, education, and social capital. Improving the negotiating position of workers and limiting the market power of giant companies will help, but in a system that leaves people to sink or swim on the basis of their ability to sell their own labor, too many will struggle to keep above water. We should certainly try to influence the way markets function so that ordinary people realize a larger share of the benefits of growth, but this will not be a complete solution for the economic insecurity faced by working people today.

In the end, a Democratic Party traumatized by the Reagan Revolution and defined by its aversion to the words "socialist" and even "liberal" has proven powerless against the economic and political forces that have created this Second Gilded Age of monumental inequality. Flattered by its growing proximity with the economic elite and unwilling to do anything that might smack of class warfare, the party that was supposed to stand up for the working class instead took the side of markets and the overall economy, protesting that this was, in fact, the smarter, more sophisticated way to help all Americans. It wasn't.

CHAPTER 3

Bad Politics

The first question is, "How is what you're selling unique?"
—Don Draper, in *Mad Men*[84]

Marketing is something that everyone thinks he or she is an expert in. We may not know how to design or build a computer, we may not have the guts to try to sell a million dollars' worth of software to a large company, but we all know a good tagline or a bad television commercial when we see it. I know this because I worked in marketing for most of my time in the business world, which meant that most of my colleagues thought (perhaps with good reason) that they could do my job as well as I could.

I don't often write about my business experience. It just isn't that relevant to most questions of economics, policy, or politics—no matter what Ross Perot, George W. Bush, Michael Bloomberg, Donald Trump, and a host of businessmen-turned-politicians like to say. Building and selling a product is very different from balancing the interests of multiple constituencies to cobble together a package of policy initiatives that serve most people more or less well, while responding to external shocks and threats like recessions or hostile regimes.

There are, however, a few basic principles of marketing that apply reasonably well to the political arena. First, whatever you are selling, your message has to relate to something that your audience cares about. If you are selling expensive software systems to large companies—something I did a lot of—you need to talk about how you can improve their business or reduce their costs, not the fanciest features of your cutting-edge technology. Second, you have to differentiate yourself from your competitors. If everyone else claims that they help companies save money, you should focus on how you help them attract new customers. Third, your message has to be legitimately based on your actual product. If you try to position yourself as the reliable, bulletproof, no-risk option, you had better have the product to back it up, or the market will soon see through you. That's why Don Draper starts off by asking a budding computer entrepreneur about his product—and what is unique about it.

Once upon a time, the Democratic Party did all of these things well. In the 1930s, in the depths of the Great Depression, President Franklin Roosevelt's central theme was economic security: jobs for the unemployed and pensions for the elderly. He identified the Democrats as the party of common people, portraying the Republicans as flunkies of the rich in the pocket of Wall Street. In a 1936 speech, he listed his enemies: "business and financial monopoly, speculation, reckless banking, class antagonism, sectionalism, war profiteering." He continued, "They are unanimous in their hate for me—and I welcome their hatred."[85] And Roosevelt backed up his words with action. His first term in office saw structural regulation of the financial sector, major public works programs, and the creation of Social Security. There could be no doubt about what the Democratic Party stood for, and why you should vote for (or against) it.

In recent decades, however, our party has forgotten these core principles. Not surprisingly, we have been routinely pummeled at the polls by our opponents, up and down the ballot and all across the country. Since the 1994 election, Republicans have controlled both houses of Congress for 14 years, Democrats for only four (and that thanks to George W. Bush's catastrophic incompetence and the Iraq War). Between 2009 and 2017, Republicans captured more than 950 seats in state legislatures from Democrats, and the number of states in which they controlled the legislature grew from 14 to 32.[86] (In the 2017 and 2018 anti-Trump elections, Republicans lost about 300 seats and control of two legislatures.) On the presidential level—where Democrats have best been able to compete, thanks to occasionally charismatic nominees and the ability to match Republicans financially—we lost the unlosable elections of 2000 and 2016, when the hand-picked successors of popular presidents, running in favorable economic environments, somehow made the contest close enough that the Electoral College mattered. And these dismal results came even as the Republicans drifted further to the right and further away from a voting public whose expressed preferences on health care, taxes, immigration, and even "cultural" issues such as gay marriage are closer to the Democrats.

The most striking example of bad political marketing in recent years, of course, was the 2016 presidential election. There are many reasons why Donald Trump defeated Hillary Clinton, including his exploitation of anti-immigrant, anti-female, and anti-minority sentiments among part of the electorate. We have to remember, however, that most Americans are not xenophobic, misogynistic, and racist, and Trump's embrace of these positions should not have been a winning strategy. While Clinton was unmistakably the candidate of tolerance and diversity (as well as basic human decency, respect for the facts, and facility with the English language), what made the election close in the first place was her inability to explain to ordinary voters what her administration would actually do for them.

Hillary Clinton's basic promise was to make the economy "work for everyone" and to "drive growth that's strong, fair, and lasting." Political campaigns are shifting targets, so I will focus here on a major speech she gave in June 2016 to lay out her economic vision.[87] Her plan focused on five key points:

1. Create better jobs.
2. Make college debt-free.
3. Change regulations to encourage corporations to pay their employees more and deter them from shifting jobs or profits overseas.
4. Increase taxes on corporations and the rich, in particular by eliminating the tax break for carried interest and implementing the "Buffett rule" (which would impose a minimum overall tax rate on the wealthy).
5. "Put families first" by providing paid family leave and better employment benefits.

As policy, these are all decent ideas. As politics, they miss the mark—beginning with the fact that three of her five points were really broad headings that encompassed laundry lists of actual ideas. (In her speech, her plan to create better jobs included 22 different policy proposals, by my count.) A platform oriented around "growth" for "everyone" is too broad to address anyone's most important concerns. How many people sitting at the kitchen table late at night, wondering how to pay the bills, think to themselves, "If only the economy would grow faster"? With the exception of debt-free college—a position Clinton was pushed into by the popularity of the Bernie Sanders campaign—and paid family leave, her proposals did not promise to solve the concrete problems of working- and middle-class Americans today. People who have jobs but struggle with rising rents or medical bills are unlikely to see how raising taxes on hedge fund managers or investing in broadband infrastructure is likely to help them.

In addition, Clinton failed to explain how her vague promise to create more higher-paying jobs was better than (or even significantly different from) the Republicans' perpetual promise to create more higher-paying jobs by cutting taxes and eliminating regulations. Her talking points included investing in infrastructure, encouraging "advanced manufacturing," improving access to credit for small businesses by "slashing unnecessary regulations" on banks, "freeing entrepreneurs to do what they do best," and providing tax credits to encourage private-sector investment and apprenticeship programs—in other words, a long catalog of nudges to try to get profit-seeking businesses to hire a few more people at somewhat higher wages. Once she conceded that all good things come from markets and the private sector, all Clinton could argue was that she would be a better economic manager than Trump—probably true, but hardly compelling. Even in a speech about the economy, her most effective means of differentiating herself from her opponent was invoking demographic issues—immigration reform, systemic racism, equal pay for women, and gay rights.

After the 2016 debacle laid bare the failure of the party to address ordinary Americans' economic concerns, the Democratic leadership promised to develop a new platform that would, in the words of Senate Minority Leader Chuck Schumer, "show the country that we're the party on the side of working people."[88] The campaign they rolled out under the headline "A Better Deal," however, was so broad as to be meaningless. "We stand for three simple things," Schumer pledged: "First, we're going to increase people's pay. Second, we're going to reduce their everyday expenses. And third, we're going to provide workers with the tools they need for the 21st-century economy." Party spokespeople, afraid to say anything that might turn away any potential voter, somehow managed to avoid differentiating the Democratic Party from the most toxic presidential administration in American history.

"We want to be in a position to help create 10 million good-paying, full-time jobs," Representative Cheri Bustos of Illinois, one of the designers of A Better Deal, said in one meeting to pitch newspaper editors. "There are still people hurting, and I think we need to acknowledge that and say that we want to do something about that." Chuck Sweeny, a reporter, answered, "Donald Trump says that too. He says exactly the same thing. Too many people are still out of work. You know, we need to do something about bringing back jobs."[89] Bustos even went on to argue for lowering the corporate tax rate—at the time, one of Trump's few coherent proposals—to which Sweeney responded, "Once again, I have no idea what the Democratic Party actually stands for anymore." Nor does anyone else.

The Democrats did win a majority of the House of Representatives in 2018 (while losing two seats in the Senate), but they did so largely by ignoring A Better Deal and riding a wave of anti-Trump resentment that had been seeking an outlet for two years. When it came to economic issues, their most potent weapon was an old-fashioned defense of a federal entitlement: in this case, protections for people with preexisting conditions.

The 2018 elections proved that Democrats can still put up a fight when Republicans go after popular government programs. But the first major weakness of the Democratic economic platform in recent decades has been a failure to talk about the economic issues that most people actually care about. Presidents Obama and Clinton liked nothing more than invoking the soaring rhetoric of growth and opportunity. Schumer, Bustos, and the rest of the leadership seem to think that repeating the word "jobs" will enable them to connect with the working class. But for most people, growth and opportunity are just abstract concepts, and jobs are not what keep them up late at night. Few people setting aside their medical bills because they are afraid to open them think that a larger economy will be the solution to their problems, or that cheaper student loans will turn their lives around. Nor are jobs the answer to all problems. For one thing, the unemployment rate is historically low; it was less than 5 percent when Donald Trump was elected president, and has since fallen as low as 3.5 percent.[90] It is true that many people have given up on looking for jobs and are not counted in those figures (although the broadest measure of unemployment, which includes discouraged and underemployed workers, is also at the lowest level since 2000[91]). But workers without the skills to find employment in a highly favorable labor market are unlikely to think that the existence of more job openings will magically make them better off. The economy has been growing for a decade, and unemployment is low, yet tens of millions of people still face a daily struggle to make ends meet.

People have real economic anxieties: the cost of health care and the prospect of illness; paying for their children's education; finding a place where they can afford to live; or not being able to retire. In recent decades, mainstream Democrats have responded by promising that growth, jobs, and prosperity would solve all of these pocketbook concerns. Of course, it is logically true that if someone makes more money, she will have more to spend on health care, education, housing, or retirement. But speaking in vague generalities is not the way to convince voters that you understand and will address the challenges that they face, especially when ordinary Americans who have lived through the past 40 years can see that prosperity has largely passed them by.

In 2000, for example, the centerpiece of Al Gore's economic platform was his promise to maintain budget surpluses and use them to pay down the national debt. While this may have been a sound policy, as politics it appealed only to a handful of policy wonks and, perhaps, the bond traders President Clinton had complained about. More generally, the desire to be seen as fiscally responsible, market-oriented centrists—and not as architects of the welfare state—has constrained Democrats' ability to say anything compelling on the subjects people care about most. Instead, the party line on education has been increased accountability and competition from charter schools; on housing, relaxing constraints on financial institutions to stimulate the mortgage market; and on retirement, incentives to help people save in private accounts sold by the asset management industry. The one exception has been health care, which both Bill Clinton and Barack Obama made the centerpiece of their initial presidential campaigns. While both were willing to offer a new federal program, in both cases they took care to highlight the role of markets and private insurers.

Ironically, some of the Democratic Party's greatest political successes have come when it has posed as the defender of the welfare state. Recall the government shutdowns of 1995–1996, which President Clinton successfully framed as a battle to defend Medicare; the resounding defeat of President George W. Bush's 2005 campaign to privatize Social Security; the 2012 electoral wins following Paul Ryan's proposal to privatize Medicare; and the 2018 defense of the Affordable Care Act. While a relentless focus on preexisting conditions helped win in the House, the strategy of playing to the middle to hold onto vulnerable Senate seats in red states largely failed. Moderates such as Joe Donnelly and Heidi Heitkamp thought that collaborating with Republicans on a 2018 financial deregulation bill would win themselves points for sensible bipartisanship, only to be soundly defeated in November.

Politically speaking, nothing suits Democratic politicians quite so well as a Republican attack on a major entitlement program, which enables them to take up arms on behalf of the common man. And yet they are mortally afraid of proposing anything that might sound like an expansion of those programs and the size of the federal government. The Democrats' defensive crouch of protecting entitlement programs can win an election here and there, but taking an emphatic stand for comprehensive economic security would build the party's brand as the champion of the ordinary voter.

The second fundamental flaw in our economic messaging is that it fails Don Draper's uniqueness test. The current Democratic Party's economic platform, boiled down to its essence, is that sound management of market capitalism will promote growth, bringing jobs and prosperity to everyone. This is scarcely distinguishable from the Republican platform, which is that market capitalism will promote growth, bringing jobs and prosperity to everyone. (Did you catch the difference?) Worse, the Republican story is better. It is simpler, more memorable, and more intuitive. For the past half-century, the conservative mantra has been unchanged: Government suppresses innovation and entrepreneurship, so minimizing taxes and regulation will unleash the power of free markets and generate prosperity for everyone. Regardless of whether this is true, it's easy to understand and communicate in memorable sound bites.

Cowed by the potent symbolism of this story, Democrats have been afraid to stand up for the importance of collective action, instead conceding that market capitalism is the answer to all economic problems and that the role of government is to support the private sector. We attempt to distinguish ourselves from Republican zealots by displaying our superior understanding of economics; because markets are prone to failures (externalities, adverse selection, moral hazard, and so on), we argue, smart government policies are necessary to make them run optimally and maximize social welfare. Plus, we continue, the Republicans are actually incompetent hypocrites who run up spending on foreign wars, while Democrats are the most prudent stewards of the national balance sheet.

Everything we say may be true. Smart public policy can improve market functioning, and Republican administrations in recent decades have been associated with lower economic growth and higher deficits (to say nothing of the tax cut–fueled disaster that was Sam Brownback's tenure as governor of Kansas). But none of that matters, as far as marketing—and hence politics—is concerned. The conservative Republican credo is passionate, unequivocal, and inspiring: Give people liberty, and they will do great things. By comparison, the Democratic response is derivative, intellectual, and patronizing: Unregulated markets generally produce good outcomes, but not always, and that's why narrowly tailored government interventions are necessary to make people better off … if anyone is still paying attention. We keep expecting the electorate to reward us for our greater intellectual refinement and our ability to use empirical evidence correctly, forgetting that voters don't care about such things.

The feebleness of our economic message is particularly apparent today. President Trump's story of how he will make the economy great again is simple: stop immigrants from stealing Americans' jobs, negotiate new trade deals that will enable us to "defeat" our trade partners, eliminate government regulations that stifle companies, and cut taxes to stimulate innovation and industry. The Democratic response is that immigrants help the economy, trade barriers hurt all countries involved, markets need regulation, and the optimal tax rate is actually higher than current levels. Again, we may be right on all counts, but at best we have captured the overeducated intellectual vote. We have forgotten that while membership in the reality-based community can help win votes against an outrageous target like President Trump, on its own it cannot generate the political support necessary to roll back decades of rightward drift and stem the rising tide of inequality.

The core problem is that we have let ourselves be maneuvered onto the enemy's home turf. Once both sides agree that the sole source of prosperity is the private sector, Republicans can keep repeating their one, easily understandable talking point: get government out of the way and let capitalism flourish. (Or, as former House Majority Leader Dick Armey said, "The market is rational and the government is dumb."[92]) Democrats can't offer anything equally bold for two reasons. First, having accepted the basic premise that markets know best, all we have to offer are nudges that try to get those markets to behave a little bit better than they currently do. Even the best-designed nudges—say, automatic enrollment in 401(k) plans—are limited in what they can achieve and are ill suited to galvanize voters. Second, our insistence that everything must be budget-neutral—based on our profound fear of being seen as fiscally irresponsible—prevents us from using the one powerful political weapon in the traditional left-wing arsenal: the promise of a bold new program. Even the Green New Deal—which is urgently needed in order to, among other things, protect the continued existence of our species —continues to be opposed and undermined by centrist Democrats. ("There's no way to pay for it," Senator Dianne Feinstein said in a hostile lecture to … 15 children.[93])

On this battleground, we cannot win. If you look at the typical profile of the candidates that Democratic congressional leaders like to recruit and support, it's almost as if they are admitting that fact. For the last decade, the prototype has been people with compelling personal profiles—particularly veterans with combat experience in Afghanistan or Iraq—strong fundraising potential, and inoffensive, middle-of-the-road policy ideas, particularly on economic issues. Looking ahead to 2020, Rahm Emanuel—President Obama's first chief of staff and a leading power broker in the party—listed "authenticity, credibility, and viability" as the key ingredients to defeating President Trump, with scarcely a mention of standing for anything in particular.[94]

American conservatives discovered long ago that the way to effect real, long-term change is to come up with bold ideas on issues that people care about and champion them passionately and persistently until the country moves in your direction. We Democrats may consider those conservative ideas to be crazy. But instead of offering bold ideas of our own, we continue to muddle through, trying to squeak out one election victory at a time by offending as few people as possible.

The Democratic Party could start talking about the real economic problems that American families face today. And we could come up with a message that clearly differentiates us from the Republicans. Some politicians already have. But the third failing of our political strategy will take much longer to fix.

It is a widespread belief that marketing is the same thing as advertising: coming up with catchy slogans and images that induce people to buy something. This notion is especially prevalent in that peculiar branch of marketing known as politics. In this age of "low information" voters, the story goes, a candidate need only figure out what different groups adding up to 51 percent of the electorate want—through surveys and focus groups—and then promise them that. Winning politicians are those who can identify key themes that resonate with voters and boil them down into powerful sound bites (of which "Build the wall" is the latest example). The losers fail to come up with the right message, or they change their message too often, or they can't deliver their message effectively.

But, as discussed above, this isn't how marketing works. Marketing begins with understanding what your target customers want—and then building it. It wasn't the "Think different" campaign, brilliant as it was, that rescued Apple from oblivion in the late 1990s and early 2000s. What mattered was that the company introduced the iMac, OS X, the iPod, and the iTunes Store within less than five years. Without excellent products that people wanted to buy, billboards featuring Muhammad Ali, Mahatma Gandhi, and Pablo Picasso would have become just another failed gimmick deserving a brief footnote in advertising history. Spending lots of money on a flashy campaign will get you attention and perhaps a short-term bump in sales, but if you can't deliver the goods, the market will eventually see through your pitch. In general, great brands have to be built on a foundation of great products, and they have to be consistent with the way people perceive those products. That's why

"Think different" worked for Apple but would have flopped for IBM, whose reputation is based on reliability, dependability, and conservatism.

Once upon a time, the Democratic Party successfully marketed a powerful brand as the advocate of workers and the middle class against the privileged elite. That brand was the consequence of things that Democratic leaders actually did for ordinary families, from Social Security and jobs programs in the 1930s through Medicare, Medicaid, and food stamps in the 1960s. The popularity of those policies and the consistency of the image they projected were the foundation for the party's nearly uninterrupted reign over Congress from the Great Depression until the Reagan Revolution. Over those decades, the party built up a deep reservoir of trust—of brand loyalty—among lower- and middle-class families. They might disagree with certain policies or dislike specific electoral candidates, but they continued to identify Democrats as the party of the New Deal and Social Security, of workers' rights and pensions and health care. The Republicans, by contrast, were the party of local notables who owned real-estate agencies and car dealerships and sat on bank boards, and of rich executives who occupied corner offices and socialized at country clubs.

After losing both the Senate and the White House in 1980, however, and especially after Walter Mondale's crushing defeat four years later, the Democratic elite no longer wanted to be associated with the poor or with workers, or at least not the unionized factory workers who had once symbolized the party. Instead, the New Democrats decided to become the party of finance, technology, and a brave new world in which the magic of markets would deliver prosperity to everyone, as told in Chapter 1. For the most part, the party has successfully expanded its appeal to these new constituencies; today, Silicon Valley and the Southern California entertainment industry are largely Democratic, and Wall Street is no longer the Republican enclave it once was. As the Republicans have increasingly espoused racism, sexism, and xenophobia,

Democrats have also responded by becoming the party of immigration, racial and ethnic minorities, gay rights, and women's rights. Tolerance and diversity are important values, and it is good that at least one party is willing to stand up for them (although, as on other issues, national Democrats did not embrace marriage equality until pushed into it by the courts and by their constituents). But they became the brand of contemporary Democrats by flowing into the vacuum left by the party's abandonment of its traditional economic identity.

At the same time that they tried to reposition themselves as forward-looking, compassionate, demographically diverse capitalists, however, Democratic candidates wanted to hold onto the votes of the poor and the working class. By definition, people making less than the median income can cast half the votes in any election, making them an important constituency. So the political balancing act of establishment Democrats from Bill Clinton forward has been cozying up to elites—and taking their cash by the bushel—while loudly proclaiming their affection for the common man and woman. (The latest installment in this story is 2020 presidential candidates—including Joe Biden, Kamala Harris, but particularly Pete Buttigieg—holding fundraisers for wealthy donors virtually in secret while touting their small-dollar donations in public.[95]) The first Clinton was the master of the genre. With his friendly Southern drawl, his immense charisma, and his modest origins—born to a single mother in a rural town called Hope—he could make peace with Wall Street, sign a draconian welfare reform bill, cut taxes on investment income, and still pass as a man of the people.

With each successive decade, however, the magic act has become harder to pull off. Struggling to pull away from the mediocre George W. Bush in 2000, Al Gore promised to fight for "those who need a voice, those who need a champion, those who need to be lifted up, so they are never left behind."[96] Unlike Clinton, however, Gore was born and grew up in Washington, D.C., son of a congressman and future senator, and the spark never passed. John Kerry, a Boston Brahmin who married into the Heinz Ketchup family, hardly tried to reach out to the masses, preferring to run as a military man and a competent civil servant.

Barack Obama had both the political gifts and the personal narrative—as a mixed-race child raised by a single mother—to cast the Clinton spell. In 2008, he was enough of a blank slate for people to project their hopes and dreams onto him, enabling him to combine a vaguely technocratic, centrist platform with a shining evocation of a better future for all people. In 2012, Obama's campaign successfully played the populist card by characterizing Mitt Romney, a private equity magnate, as the ruthless boss who lays you off. By contrast, Hillary Clinton was widely perceived as immensely rich and accustomed to the corridors of power. The awkward spectacle of her paid speeches to Wall Street financiers—and her steadfast refusal to tell the public what she had actually said—highlighted the immense difficulty she faced in appealing to the working-class voters who were once the bedrock of her party.

Clinton still won a majority of votes from people in households with incomes less than $50,000 per year. But Donald Trump won *16* percentage points more than Mitt Romney had four years earlier among people making less than $30,000; he did six points better among those making between $30,000 and $50,000. He won 78 percent of the votes of people who said their family's financial situation was worse than four years before—people facing economic insecurity who once would have naturally turned to Democrats.[97] Compared to Romney, Trump did better in counties suffering economic distress, particularly in the (post-)industrial Midwest, both rural and urban; he won in places like Trumbull County, Ohio, where real median household income fell by 27 percent since 1980, and which voted for Obama twice by more than 20 percentage points.[98] In general, Trump did better in counties with lower (or negative) gains in median incomes and employment levels.[99]

He also did especially well in counties that were vulnerable to competition from imports from China.[100]

One could argue that, whatever Clinton's weaknesses as a candidate, low- and middle-income voters should still have recognized that she would better serve their interests than Donald Trump, who was promising to repeal the Affordable Care Act and shower the rich with yet another major tax cut. But the underlying problem was that the historical Democratic brand—the party of the workers and ordinary people, not corporate executives and the rich—had withered away due to years of neglect. In politics, as in business, brands don't last forever. Lincoln freed the slaves, and, for almost a century, African Americans were largely loyal to the Republican Party. Then Lyndon Johnson embraced the civil rights movement, Richard Nixon's Southern strategy drew in formerly Democratic whites unhappy with desegregation, and soon the party of Lincoln had become the party of racial resentment.

Bill Clinton inherited a brand image that had been built up over decades, as Democratic presidents and congressional majorities actually did things that helped the working class, often at the expense of the rich, who paid higher taxes to fund a larger government and a broader safety net. That image was a major reason why Clinton could sustain his popularity with lower-income voters despite not doing anything in particular to help them. The popular identification of the Democratic Party with ordinary people of modest means survived into this century, even as the party's elected representatives did little to justify it. But by 2016, the credit built up by Franklin Roosevelt and Lyndon Johnson had been completely drawn down. Unemployed factory workers, underpaid service industry employees, single mothers struggling to find child care, retirees stretching their Social Security checks to cover their prescriptions—at some point they stopped trusting that the Democratic Party would do anything for them or even cared about them. They may not have wholeheartedly embraced the Republicans, but they didn't turn out to support Democrats, particularly in the states that were decisive in the 2016 election.

It is true that American voters are not particularly well informed about economic issues and what policies are best for them and for the country. But you can only fool people for so long, and certainly not for a quarter-century. The marketing remained the same: Democrats would "fight for you" or restore "power to the people" or give you a "better deal" or some such collection of words. But the product itself changed during those years, to the point where it could no longer support the message. In the 2016 presidential election, for the first time in modern history, the Democratic candidate did better among high-income voters (the top 10 percent by income) than among everyone else.[101] Today, many in the party want to take up the cause of antitrust and pose as the scourge of big business. But few people will believe it as long as congressional leaders continue doing the bidding of monopolies like Facebook, which counts Minority Leader Schumer among its most powerful supporters.[102] If Democrats have a brand identity today, it is as the party of tolerance, multiculturalism, and women's rights, all of which are important causes. But it is no longer the party of the economically less fortunate, regardless of what its politicians claim.

By adopting the central Republican idea that dynamic markets and limited government are the sole source of prosperity, we lost the ability to differentiate our economic message from our opponents'. By forgoing bold programs to help struggling families directly and doing nothing to slow the progress of extreme inequality, we squandered our brand equity and our greatest political asset. Yes, we can still win elections by combining attractive candidate biographies with important themes such as women's rights and climate change, while hoping that voters will be repelled by Republican bigotry and corruption. But when it comes to the basic economic issues that still play a large role in dictating election outcomes, we have a lousy product and no real message at all.

In tacking toward the middle and trying to be all things to all people—defenders of the 99 percent *and* enablers of the 1 percent—Democrats have also forgotten the cardinal lesson of modern American political history. In the 1950s, conservatism was completely impotent as an ideology in the United States. There was a Republican Party, but its economic platform amounted to little more than accommodation to the New Deal and a vague claim to fiscal responsibility. Its leader, President Dwight Eisenhower, famously wrote:

> Should any political party attempt to abolish Social Security, unemployment insurance, and eliminate labor laws and farm programs, you would not hear of that party again in our political history. There is a tiny splinter group, of course, that believes you can do these things. … Their number is negligible and they are stupid.[103]

Eisenhower also believed exactly what Democrats today believe: that government action was necessary to correct for the failings of the private sector. His compelling personal story as the conquering general of World War II got him by, but did little for the Republican brand.

Sixty years later, extreme conservatives have completely reshaped the political landscape. They have increasingly tightened their stranglehold on the Republican Party; they have lowered taxes and cut back regulations to an extent their ancestors could only have dreamed of; they have slashed welfare (with President Clinton's assistance) and put privatization of Social Security and Medicare onto the national agenda; they have installed a generation of judges who are determined to restore pre–New Deal limits on the powers of the federal government; and, as discussed above, they have dragged the Democratic Party so far to the right that it occupies the space once taken by mainstream Republicans. They have accomplished all this despite positions on immigration, race, women's rights, and gay rights that are offensive to a majority of the population.

They did it not by adapting their identity to what the median voter wanted, but by staking out compelling positions on core issues (most importantly, that small government and free markets are the source of prosperity) and repeating their key messages incessantly until the electorate came to them. They did it while rallying around Barry Goldwater in 1964 even though he had no chance at winning the general election, backing Ronald Reagan's 1976 challenge to a sitting Republican president, and purging their congressional delegation of moderate incumbents better positioned to hold onto seats for their party.

By contrast, in recent elections—particularly since 1992—Democrats have run toward the middle, desperately trying to please the crucial swing demographic of the moment, whatever it may be. That's why the national party was opposed to or silent on gay marriage until state-level momentum was impossible to ignore, why it tiptoed around abortion (largely supporting restrictions on federal funding for abortions) until only the last few years, and why it still has an equivocal position on climate change and the fossil fuel industry, to cite only a few issues. That's why the ideal candidate recruited by the Democratic Congressional or Senatorial Campaign Committee is a combat veteran who started a small business and now promises to get Washington to work creating jobs and opportunity—without saying anything that might sound like redistribution, expanding the welfare state, or raising taxes on the rich. While conservatives demand ideological purity, the Democratic establishment silences its left wing and extols the political virtues of centrism (while its presidential candidates fantasize about a mythical post-partisan America). To us, every election is so crucial, every swing voter so important, that the priority is always to grind out a win by catering to any bloc of undecideds or independents necessary—rather than spelling out a clear vision of where we are headed and asking the people to come with us.

But the joke is on us. While we have been eagerly cozying up to the median voter, the conservatives have been remaking the American economy. They have cut taxes, undermined the safety net, slashed "job-killing" regulations, turned federal agencies over to the industries they are supposed to monitor, promoted the extraction of fossil fuels, stacked the judiciary with pro-business judges, and so on—sometimes (as with welfare reform, financial deregulation, and shale gas drilling) abetted by Democrats anxious to seem "pro-business" or simply hopeful for campaign contributions or plum lobbying jobs. If you look at how the landscape of national politics has changed since 1980, it is clear who won and who lost, at least when it comes to economic issues. The Republicans don't win every election or every vote—although from 2010 through 2016, it often seemed that way—but that is because they have moved the terrain of political debate so far in their direction. We don't have to endorse their substantive positions, or their often cavalier disregard for facts, to appreciate that the conservative minority has executed the most powerful, long-running political marketing campaign of our lifetimes.

The most important lesson of the conservative revolution is that real change takes time. It took decades of centrist policies to undermine the Democratic brand, and it will take decades to restore it. But the sooner we begin, the better.

CHAPTER 4

Our Democratic Party

We cannot be all things to all people. We have to determine which side of history we are on.
　　—Jesse Jackson, 1989[104]

　　The Democratic Party needs an economic message. We need voters to identify our brand with something they care about. We need to differentiate ourselves from the Republican mantra that free markets are the source of all good things. And we need a story with substance behind it—not a warm mush of empty, focus group–tested slogans that bear no relation to the policies we actually pursue. If we simply announce that we care about Main Street and not Wall Street, no one will believe us—with reason, given our recent history. We need to earn back the trust of ordinary people by building an economic strategy that will help them and using whatever power we have to make it a reality.

Good marketing makes a credible promise to give people something that they need or want—to help them realize their dreams, solve their problems, or alleviate their fears. Unfortunately, when it comes to the economic climate of the contemporary United States, the dominant emotion is fear. More than 60 percent of adults are worried about keeping their health care coverage, paying their medical bills, and saving enough for retirement; more than three-quarters are afraid that today's children will be worse off than their parents. Americans think it is harder to "get ahead" than in previous generations, and are pessimistic about the opportunities that young people today will have in the future.[105]

These fears are justified. The hard-working, law-abiding citizens who make up a large majority of our country face a degree of economic insecurity unworthy of a supposedly rich nation. After decades in which ordinary incomes have barely kept up with inflation, workers have no reason to believe that their economic fortunes will necessarily improve. Many adults, trapped by the rising costs of health care, education, and housing, have failed to amass any significant savings. As of 2016, the typical middle-income family had less than $19,000 in financial assets, not counting retirement plans—and $42,000 in debt (which might be secured by a nonfinancial asset, like a house). Since the 1980s, median debt levels have increased by at least two-thirds (after adjusting for inflation) for families of all income levels and all ages.[106] An analysis by the Pew Charitable Trusts found that more than two-thirds of households are financially strained by meager savings, insufficient income, or high debt payments.[107] It is no surprise that only one-half of adults think that they could stave off serious financial difficulty for more than two months if they lost their jobs.[108] According to a report by the Federal Reserve, two in five people would be unable to cover an unexpected expense of only $400 (such as a minor automobile repair) without having to borrow money or sell something; 12 percent could not afford the $400 under any circumstances; one in four skipped needed medical care in the past year because of cost; and only one in three people in the workforce think they are saving enough for retirement.[109] This is true after a decade of economic expansion and historically low unemployment.

Signs of economic insecurity are everywhere around us. There is the increasing popularity of "gig" work, most notably driving for Uber and Lyft. There are the ubiquitous advertisements for college and graduate degrees—many offered by for-profit institutions—with pictures of shiny new careers. There are the constant robocalls and advertisements promising to refinance student loans or consolidate credit card debt. Insecurity is not limited to the poor and the working class. Year-to-year income instability has grown for all segments of society, including the middle class and the highly educated.[110]

Among the more affluent, insecurity is reflected in the collective mania over college admissions. Once upon a time, a four-year degree from a state university was a reasonable guarantee of a secure and comfortable place in the upper middle class; today, as the very rich are jetting off into a rarefied social stratum all to themselves, parents are panicked that their children will be left behind, and some have even taken to cheating their way into ensuring them a place at a prestigious private university.

One way to address people's fears, regrettably, is to encourage them to blame someone else: immigrants, minorities, Chinese workers, or a shadowy cabal of international politicians and financiers. We've seen how that works. But that is not the only way.

Instead, we can show people that we understand their fears and the real problems on which they are based, and offer them concrete solutions that directly address their most important anxieties. It was enough for Bill Clinton to "feel your pain," but a quarter-century of rising inequality later, voters are looking for more than eloquent sympathy. The more that people worry about negative shocks such as job losses and medical emergencies, the more they tend to support government policies specifically aimed at cushioning people against economic insecurity.[111]

Vague promises of growth and opportunity—the credo of the Democratic elite from Clinton to Obama to Clinton—are too nebulous and speculative for people struggling with rising rents in desirable cities, student loan debt incurred at fraudulent for-profit universities, or out-of-network charges not covered by their health care plans. The fundamental problem with the growth-and-opportunity doctrine—the reason why it has failed in recent decades—is inequality. Contemporary global capitalism has produced a winner-take-all society in which a shrinking elite, composed of the highly skilled and highly fortunate (and their children and descendants), monopolizes an inexorably increasing share of the fruits of our collective efforts. There are many factors behind this economic transformation—technology, global markets and supply chains, free capital flows, corporate concentration, and financialization, to name a few. We could attempt to constrain some of these forces through regulation, but many are far beyond the control of any national legislature.

Contemporary Democrats like Barack Obama respond to inequality of wealth or income by talking about equality of opportunity. That makes them sound like market-oriented capitalists, not socialists. But the policies they suggest, while laudable—more funding for public schools, cheaper student loans, job retraining programs, lending to small businesses—are so woefully inadequate to level the economic playing field that you have to wonder if they are at all serious. The advantages of being born into the economic and educational elite (and of being the right race and gender) vastly dwarf any moderately ambitious policy to help the less fortunate. Socioeconomic mobility—the potential for people to move up (or down) in the income distribution—has long been lower in the United States than in other advanced economies, and by most measures has declined since the 1970s.[112]

True equality of opportunity would require a degree of social engineering that would be unfathomable today, such as a 100 percent estate tax, random assignment of students to schools, and probably even some kind of shared parenting system. And what then? The logic of capitalism would continue to produce extreme inequality; we would still live in a society of the 1 percent and the 99 percent, only one with a less morally objectionable starting point. Giving disadvantaged people *better* opportunities is of course a good thing. But the solution cannot be simply that we will help people compete a little more effectively in a contest where a select few take the spoils and everyone else shares the crumbs.

The flip side of an economy that showers its winners with unprecedented rewards is that the perils of losing are greater than in previous generations: a lifetime of insecurity for a stagnant material standard of living. Our answer cannot be that increased opportunity will make us all better off. We have all known since elementary school that not everyone can be a winner, and decades of rising inequality have only reinforced the lesson. Both Barack Obama and Hillary Clinton liked to talk about "ladders of opportunity"; but in the 2016 election, those metaphorical ladders "fell far short of what real people were looking for," according to Stan Greenberg, a longtime friend and ally of the Clintons (and onetime pollster for the Democratic Leadership Council). "Incomes sagged after the financial crisis, pensions lost value, and many lost their housing wealth, while people faced dramatically rising costs for things that mattered—health care, education, housing, and child care."[113]

Instead of insisting that all people need is an opportunity, our economic strategy should focus on guaranteeing that all Americans can enjoy the indispensable requirements of a 21st-century life, without living in constant fear of a layoff, a medical emergency, or an auto breakdown. Our message should be that a civilized society ensures the basic well-being of all of its members. Capitalism and growth are not ends in themselves, but means to an end: the welfare of all people.

But a message alone is not enough; no marketing campaign can be better than the products that it is trying to sell. For the Democratic Party, the products need to be policies that directly target the key sources of insecurity faced by ordinary American families. We need compelling solutions for four key challenges that millions of people struggle with every day: health care, education, housing, and retirement. Not only are these basic necessities, but out-of-pocket medical expenses, college tuition, and rents have all climbed rapidly in recent decades, squeezing household budgets, while the shift away from traditional pensions has left more and more people dreading retirement. There may be other things that you want to add to this list, but this is where we need to start. Bold programs to solve these challenges will make a huge differ-ence in reducing economic uncertainty for almost everyone—and will re-establish the Democratic Party as the party of the people.

Health Care

The argument is now so familiar that it hardly needs explanation. The only long-term solution to our fundamental health care problems is Medicare for All—a system in which the federal government provides basic health insurance to all Americans. As discussed in Chapter 1, all politicians say that they want decent care at an affordable price for everyone, so whether you live or die does not depend on your income. Obamacare uses a complex set of regulations to attempt to force private markets (against their natural inclinations) to produce this desirable outcome. But what people say they want is actually a perfect descrip-tion of a single-payer system in which everyone gets the same policy with a basic set of benefits, and financial contributions—via some combination of payroll taxes, income-based premiums (such as those for Medicare Part B), and general revenues (primarily the individual income tax)—are based on the ability to pay. The new system should improve on Medicare, in particular by placing limits on annual out-of-pocket spending, which already exist for Obamacare plans. Medicare for All need not eliminate private insurance; insurers (and employers) could offer policies providing additional benefits. Because coverage would no longer be contingent on employment, it would be easier for people to make choices in the job market. Compared to Obamacare, Medicare for All is a simpler, fairer, more effective way of reaching what everyone claims to be the desired outcome.

Just as important, a single-payer system would not share Obamacare's fatal flaw: its dependence on market competition to control costs. In the long term, the bigger problem we face is not that we have a poorly designed insurance system, but that we are paying more and more for health care relative to everything else in the economy. In recent years, as prices charged by providers have continued to rise, insurers have resorted to some combination of increasing premiums, imposing greater cost-sharing on policyholders, and restricting their provider networks (creating the growing problem of uncovered out-of-network services). The federal government, by contrast, has the market power to simply dictate reimbursement rates to doctors and hospitals, which is the only sure way to keep costs under control. Constraining reimbursements could mean that doctors, hospitals, pharmaceutical companies, and device manufacturers will make less money, but they will still likely earn more than in comparable countries.

A common argument against Medicare for All is that it would be too expensive. This is a fallacy. It is true that a single-payer system would significantly expand the federal budget because a larger share of our overall health care spending would flow through the government. That increased spending, however, can be funded simply by diverting the money that we currently pay to the health care industry. Instead of paying premiums to insurers every month, along with co-pays and deductibles and out-of-network charges, the population as a whole would pay roughly the same amount of money to the government in the form of taxes and premiums. If anything, the aggregate cost of health insurance should be lower with single-payer because of lower administrative costs due to scale. (Medicare already has far lower costs than private insurers.) Over time, as explained above, the federal government can do a better job of holding down underlying medical costs. And a single-payer system financed by taxes makes it possible to spread the total cost of health insurance in a more equitable way, compared to the current system under which high- and low-income employees pay essentially the same amount. At the end of the day, what matters is how much we pay for health care and who pays—not whether or not that spending flows through the federal budget.

Politically, Medicare for All is also popular with a majority of all people (not just Democrats)—as high as 70 percent in some studies.[114] Phrasing matters in polls, but even the less friendly terms "national health plan" and "single-payer health insurance system" are seen more favorably.[115] Medicare for All still retains majority support even after the all-out assault against it launched by centrist Democratic presidential candidates this year.[116]

The "public option" is popular with the moderate wing of the party, because it seems to offer the best of both worlds—employer-sponsored coverage for those who can get it, and government insurance for those who can't. But it can only pull off this balancing act because its proponents have received far less scrutiny than Elizabeth Warren.[117] If—as it seems in Pete Buttigieg's plan—the public option is just another marketplace plan available on the Obamacare exchanges with the same subsidies (and perhaps slightly lower prices because of the federal government's administrative cost advantage), then it's not much of a solution for our affordability and cost control problems. To make health care affordable, a public option would have to offer superior benefits with much lower cost-sharing; to give people a real choice, it would have to allow employees to use their employers' money to pay for it; to make good coverage available for people with little money, it would have to tap deeply into general tax revenues; to control costs, it would have to have a dominant share of the market; and, at that point, it would be little different from Medicare for All.

When it comes to health care, the Democratic position should not be that we will give you one more option that you may or may not be able to afford. It should be that everyone needs health care, and everyone will get it.

Education

In the decades after World War II, a high school education was often sufficient to land a secure job with generous health and retirement benefits, at least for white men. Not so any longer. With the end of lifetime employment and the advent of the knowledge economy, a college education has become an indispensable credential in a highly competitive job market. At the same time, academically oriented preschool is increasingly perceived as a necessity rather than a luxury, especially as the understanding of its long-term benefits has grown. The old educational model, in which free, public K-12 schools fueled the growth of the American economy and swelled the ranks of the middle class, is no longer enough—which is one reason students are willing to take on unprecedented amounts of debt in pursuit of college degrees.

Yet as education has become more important in shaping people's economic fortunes, it has become less affordable and less equitable. We have the best research universities in the world and many excellent primary and secondary institutions, but we also have schools that fail to provide any kind of useful education and for-profit colleges that actively prey on students, inducing them to take on piles of debt that will take decades to repay. Good preschools are predominantly private and available only to wealthier families. At the K-12 level, the best schools tend to be the most expensive, whether elite private institutions or public schools paid for by property taxes in rich neighborhoods. Although the most selective colleges tend to be relatively affordable (because of their generous financial aid programs), places in their entering classes are effectively reserved for those able to go to an outstanding high school. As a whole, this system only exacerbates inequality by allowing the scions of the wealthy to get on the escalator of career success, while putting up barriers in front of the children of the poor.

Overhauling the K-12 sector would be a monumental task and is largely beyond the scope of the federal government, since most decisions are made by local school boards and state governments. On these levels, Democrats should at a minimum push for higher teacher pay and for equalizing school funding across districts. At the national level, however, we can take two major steps to make a comprehensive education a right for all Americans: universal public preschool and free college.

Pre-K programs (generally for children ages three and four) have received a lot of attention because of recent research showing that they can have a huge impact on measures of later achievement, including high school graduation, crime, employment, income, and health. Good early-childhood education produces high rates of return for society—that is, its long-term benefits far exceed its up-front costs.[118] Preschool is also important because it is the time when the achievement gap opens up between upper- and lower-income students—a gap that, in many cases, will never close. On average, low-income children enter kindergarten almost one year behind their higher-income peers in math and more than one year behind in reading; African American and Hispanic students also lag behind by six months to a year.[119] Although many factors are involved, one important cause of these differences is access to preschool.[120] Families making more than $100,000 per year are more than three times as likely to send children to preschool at age three as those making between $20,000 and $30,000.[121] One study estimated that a high-quality, universal pre-K program could reduce the school readiness gap between low- and high-income students by 27 percent to 41 percent, with a considerably greater impact on disparities associated with race and ethnicity—and those estimates are based on existing programs that are only one year long.[122]

Universal, full-day, public pre-K would also help alleviate the considerable financial burden of child care for working parents, many of whom cannot afford to stay home to take care of their kids. The federal government could go a long way toward this goal by providing the large majority of funds to states or localities that operate preschool programs—such as New York City and Washington, D.C., where most four-year-old children attend publicly funded pre-K.

As higher education has become more and more important in recent decades, the cost of college has climbed rapidly, and the only response from Washington has been regulatory changes that make it easier for students to borrow money at slightly lower interest rates. The result has been increasing financial burdens on families, students dropping out of school because they can't work enough jobs to make ends meet, and graduates mired in debt. Student debt has itself become a major source of financial insecurity; more than 15 percent of borrowers default within five years, and another 15 percent are severely delinquent or otherwise not making payments.[123]

Our free-college program should ensure that any qualified student can earn an undergraduate degree without having to borrow money. The federal government could match funds put up by states to eliminate tuition and fees at community colleges and public universities. In addition, Congress could expand the Pell grant program to cover additional expenses (housing, food, books, etc.) for needy students. Proposals along these lines have been put forward by Senator Brian Schatz and Representative Mark Pocan, Senator Elizabeth Warren, and Senator Bernie Sanders. They obviously increase government spending, but by less than $100 billion per year[124]—a couple of percentage points of the federal budget, or a fraction of the tax cuts signed into law by President Trump in 2017.

As with health care, the Democratic Party should take the problem of paying for preschool and college completely off the table. Universal pre-K and free college are simple, compelling ideas that are popular with the public. Americans overwhelmingly support the idea of making preschool accessible to everyone, and almost two-thirds are willing to pay more in taxes to support early-childhood education.[125] More than three-quarters of survey respondents think the federal government should "make sure that everyone who wants to go to college can do so," and a majority generally favor free college.[126]

Some naysayers prefer some form of means-testing—limiting benefits to people whose families are sufficiently poor—on the grounds that free public universities are an unnecessary handout to the wealthy (although most of the children of the rich are going to private colleges as it is). But they miss the point. Even leaving aside the greater political appeal of a universal entitlement, we live in a supposedly advanced society in which everyone should have the *right* to a comprehensive education, just as everyone should have the right to health care, and just as everyone already has the right to a K-12 education—and clean air, clean water, police protection, and so on. These are not commodities that should be distributed by markets, with the government begrudgingly stepping in to help the destitute. They are necessities of modern life that society should provide to all of its members.

Education alone is not the solution to wage stagnation and inequality. The core problem is an economic system that overwhelmingly rewards a few winners at everyone else's expense, and preparing students to compete a little better does not change that fact.[127] But while we cannot guarantee that all graduates will be able to land well-paying and rewarding jobs, we can at least eliminate the economic insecurity created by the need and desire for a quality education.

Housing

Everyone needs a place to live. All over America, finding a home is becoming an insuperable challenge for many families. As rich people make more money and cluster in desirable cities (which also have many of the best jobs), everyone else is being pushed out by rising rents. For example, the median rent for a two-bedroom apartment is $39,000 per year in Boston, $49,000 in New York City, and $54,000 in San Francisco.[128] For too long, the Democratic Party's housing strategy was scarcely distinguishable from George W. Bush's fanciful image of an "ownership society," consisting largely of deregulating the mortgage market to push the homeownership rate up a few percentage points. We all know how that turned out.

We need to recognize that buying a house with a white picket fence is not a feasible option for many of the people having the hardest time finding a place to live. We should focus instead on increasing the availability of affordable rental homes. The central problem in the rental market is that the number of reasonably priced units has not kept pace with economic growth in many metropolitan areas, as developers target affluent households—in part by converting low-rent buildings into luxury apartments. Across the country, rents have climbed by 25 percent more than prices in general since 1997.[129] As a result, almost half of all renting households have to pay more than 30 percent of their income for housing, double the proportion of the 1960s; of those, 11 million pay more than half of their income to the landlord.[130] The situation is obviously worse for families without a lot of money to begin with. For every 100 renting households making less than 30 percent of the median income in their area, there are only 46 adequate and affordable units available, even taking federal subsidies into account.[131] Not surprisingly given these conditions, more than 1 million people resort to homeless shelters at some point during the year.[132]

An affordable-housing strategy will need several components. It should begin with large increases in federal subsidies for the construction of new housing units in neighborhoods where rents are high relative to median incomes. Existing incentive programs for private-sector construction (primarily the Low-Income Housing Tax Credit) are both inefficient and far too small to meet the enormous demand for affordable housing. They should be supplemented by direct federal loans to local governments to develop and operate mixed-income public housing, building on the successful experiences of municipalities around the world.[133] Buildings financed with any public money should be required to maintain affordable rents (relative to local income levels) for several decades. Federal money should also be contingent on relaxing exclusionary zoning laws, which prop up the price of housing by limiting density while indirectly maintaining racial segregation.

Expanding supply will not be enough, however, because many families cannot afford even reasonable prices; the largest federal rental assistance program is a tax credit for developers to build affordable units, yet more than half of the tenants in those homes need additional government help to pay the rent.[134] We should expand funding for the Housing Choice Voucher Program, better known as Section 8, which currently only serves a small fraction of eligible families, with average wait times of 32 months.[135] In addition, the program's rules should be changed so that vouchers can be used in more expensive neighborhoods, and landlords should be prohibited from discriminating against participants. The federal government should also provide funding for state and local emergency rental assistance programs, which can help keep families in their homes despite short-term disruptions in their cash flow (due to medical emergencies, car problems, etc.).

The best source of funding for affordable rental housing is obvious: subsidies for homeowners, primarily the mortgage interest tax deduction and the capital gains exclusion for the sale of houses. Currently, homeowners can deduct from their taxable income the interest they pay on mortgages of up to $1 million for principal residences ($750,000 for houses bought after the 2017 tax cut). This is terrible policy for many reasons: It encourages people to take on more debt; it doesn't make it easier to buy a first house, because the tax break is already reflected in higher prices; and, worst of all, the subsidy primarily flows to the rich. The vast majority of homeowners don't deduct mortgage interest because they are better off with the standard deduction, especially after it was raised in 2017; of the people who do, those with the biggest mortgages and in the highest tax brackets benefit the most. Of the $31 billion that the federal government will give out in tax savings in 2020, 60 percent will go to households making $200,000 or more. In addition, the first $500,000 of profits on the sale of a house are exempt from capital gains tax (the tax you ordinarily pay when you sell an asset for more than you paid for it). This provision—which, again, primarily benefits people with expensive houses—will cost the federal government another $37 billion next year.[136]

Together, these two tax breaks represent $68 billion in subsidies that we are handing out to the people who need them the least, to encourage behavior (buying houses) that they would do anyway. Our message, again, should be simple and clear: We will do whatever it takes to ensure that every American family can find an affordable place to live, rather than funneling more money to the people who already have the biggest houses.

Retirement

Throughout most of human history, people did not retire, at least not in the sense of the word today. As late as 1930, almost 60 percent of men over the age of 65 were still in the workforce—at a time when life expectancy for males (at birth) was less than 60 years.[137] Most people worked more or less until they died. Social Security, created in 1935 as one of the centerpieces of the New Deal, was intended to make it possible for elderly workers—at first, largely white, male, manufacturing workers—to retire without having to live in poverty. After World War II, generous pension programs sponsored by large companies and state governments, along with Medicare, briefly made it seem as if all employees would be able to retire in relative comfort.

In recent decades, however, as the private sector largely abandoned traditional pension plans, the rhetoric of retirement security changed. Both Republicans and Democrats embraced the idea that workers should rely on 401(k) and similar accounts (invested in the booming stock market). Government became a mere creator of tax incentives (401(k), IRA, Roth IRA, SEP-IRA, and so on) and implementer of nudges (like auto-enrollment, discussed earlier) to encourage individual saving. The problem with this strategy is that it doesn't work: Even in their late fifties and early sixties, only 60 percent of families have any retirement accounts, and their median value is only $120,000.[138] Half of all households are at risk of not having enough income in retirement—compared to less than one-third in the 1980s.[139] No amount of tax breaks and clever incentives can change the basic problem: Most Americans simply don't make enough money to save for the future.

The solution is simple: We should increase Social Security benefits—rather than decreasing them, as President Obama offered in the 2011 long-term budget negotiations. It is time to recognize that, with company pensions and personal savings depleted or nonexistent, many of the elderly are completely dependent on Social Security. For one-third of recipients, it provides more than 90 percent of total income. Yet benefits are modest, averaging about $17,000 per year; the typical middle-income worker will only receive about 41 percent of his or her pre-retirement income, and will have to adjust to a significantly lower standard of living.[140]

We should increase the benefit calculation formulas and minimum benefit levels to help all retirees, but particularly those with the lowest incomes. We should also change the formula for annual cost-of-living increases so that it more accurately reflects the expenses incurred by seniors, particularly for medical care. Fortunately, this is one issue on which there is broad agreement among Democratic legislators, with multiple bills proposed in Congress along these lines (notably the Social Security 2100 Act and the Social Security Expansion Act).

There are two obvious ways to finance greater retirement benefits. One is increasing or eliminating the threshold above which income is exempt from the Social Security payroll tax ($132,900 in 2019). Getting rid of this cap would tap into the increasing share of income flowing to the wealthy, and would change the system's primary funding source from a regressive tax to a flat tax on earnings from labor. In addition, the tax could be extended to apply to investment income, at least for high-income households, similar to the Medicare payroll tax (which was expanded by the Affordable Care Act).

A second source of funding is existing tax breaks for retirement savings plans such as 401(k)s, IRAs, and Roth IRAs. The ability to deduct contributions to these accounts is supposed to encourage people to save more. In practice, however, the benefits flow largely to wealthy people who can afford to "max out" retirement account contributions, pay income tax at the highest rates, and need no incentive to save enough.[141] Eliminating these unnecessary and regressive tax preferences would free up more than $150 billion in annual revenues that could be used to fund more generous Social Security benefits for lower- and middle-income retirees.[142]

Expanding Social Security benefits is also politically popular. Large majorities of survey respondents say that they want their elected officials to increase benefits.[143] When asked how to improve the program's finances, two-thirds are in favor of raising the cap on earnings subject to the payroll tax.[144] This should come as no surprise. Although Democratic politicians have been waxing eloquent about private-sector growth and ladders of opportunity since the early 1990s, the federal government programs that people care about most are Social Security and Medicare—the traditional safety net (or welfare state, as it used to be called) that the New Democrats sought to distance themselves from. These programs were founded on the old-fashioned principle that a prosperous society should provide for the needs of its members who are no longer able to work—not that each person should be left to face the risks of old age alone, with little more than a motivational tax deduction. That is the principle that we need to reaffirm.

You may disagree with some aspects of the proposals above. That's fine. As a party, we can leave the details—whether to raise or eliminate the wage cap on the Social Security payroll tax, whether to replace the mortgage interest deduction with a refundable tax credit, and so on—for later. But we have to attack the core sources of economic insecurity with ideas that are simple, powerful, and compelling. We can't limit ourselves to safe plans that will pass muster with every subgroup across the center and the left, such as allowing the government to negotiate prescription drug prices, or using public seed money to attract private capital to invest in infrastructure. These are good ideas, but sadly insufficient to meet the demands of our time. Our goal has to be to eliminate health care, education, housing, and retirement as threats to the well-being of the vast majority of the population, and to do so directly, not by hoping we can nudge the free market into producing slightly better outcomes for slightly more people.

You may also want to add other issues to this list. That is also fine, provided that they are concrete sources of insecurity that can be directly addressed through specific proposals—not through vague encomiums to opportunity and prosperity. I don't think infrastructure should be one of the central planks of our platform, important as it may be, because few struggling families would list poor roads and bridges as an immediate source of personal worry. By contrast, a strong case can be made that a comprehensive climate strategy should be another pillar of our economic strategy. It is difficult to overestimate how concerned (and pessimistic) young people are about the world they will live in 50 years from now. A Green New Deal—including large-scale investment in renewable energies, funded by a carbon tax, and accompanied by hard limits on emissions—could go a long way toward protecting the planet and convincing younger voters that the Democratic Party does care about their future.

The Temptation of "Jobs"

Even if you agree with much of the above, you may ask: What about jobs? Shouldn't we be the party of jobs? Indeed, there is nothing that contemporary Democrats love talking about more. That way they can position themselves as advocates for ordinary people while emphasizing that they believe in capitalism and work, not socialism and redistribution.

Jobs are a good thing, and of course we should pursue policies that will help create them. But jobs alone are not enough, and there are multiple reasons why they should not be the center of our platform. As a matter of marketing, saying that we are the party of jobs, or more jobs, or better jobs, is not differentiated. The Republicans are also the party of more and better jobs, and they have a powerful story about how they will produce those jobs: cut taxes, get the government out of the way, and let American ingenuity and entrepreneurship flourish. This story may not be true, but it sure sounds good. Our narrative invariably contains more detours, because it involves the government doing something that creates the incentive for companies to hire more people or pay them more. While our story may make more economic sense, it is simply not as compelling as our opponents'.

More important, right now, creating jobs is not the problem. As of 2019, the headline unemployment rate is at its lowest level since the

1960s, and the broadest rate (including people who gave up looking for a job, and those who can't get enough hours) was only lower in 2000 at the peak of the economic boom.[145] Those jobs, however, don't pay enough to maintain a decent standard of living. The two most common occupations in America are retail salespeople (8.8 million) and food and beverage servers (7.6 million)—earning median hourly wages of $11.33 and $10.43, respectively. (Those food and beverage servers do not include another 4.2 million fast-food and counter workers, who typically make $10.32 per hour.)[146] More than 40 million people work for less than $12 per hour, which puts them right around the poverty line for a family of four.[147] As we know, there are lots of people worried about paying for health care, struggling to make the rent, or afraid they're not saving for retirement—and most of them have jobs.

Of course we should do what we can to pay people more. A $15 minimum wage is a good start—although that still only translates into $2,500 per month (obviously less for part-time jobs), or $2,309 after payroll taxes. That's less than the median rent for a two-bedroom apartment in a place like the San Francisco Bay Area. Even in economically depressed Western Massachusetts, where I live, the median rent of $1,117 would use up almost half of your paycheck.[148] We should have paid family leave, so people don't have to choose between raising their children or taking care of their parents and keeping their jobs. We should make it easier for unions to organize and to bargain for a greater share of the fruits of their labor. But with membership at only 6.4 percent of private-sector employees, it will take time for stronger unions to make a major difference for the vast majority of workers.[149] Our fundamental problem is an economy that divides everyone into winners and everyone else based on family, education, job skills, demographic characteristics, and pure luck, in which millions of people cannot reliably earn enough at work to escape constant insecurity.

Many Democrats insist that the answer should be *better* jobs. Maybe there's no way McDonald's will ever pay its employees a living wage; the front counter staff are being replaced by kiosks, and it's not hard to imagine robots taking over for the food preparers in the back. But, according to this line of thinking, the solution should be giving those people higher-skilled jobs that are more productive and therefore pay more. We do that by subsidizing companies to create those better jobs and by giving people better education, so they are able to compete for them. This is an enticing vision. Indeed, it is the core of the New Democrat response to inequality, wage stagnation, and poverty. That alone, almost three decades after Bill Clinton was elected, should give you a clue as to how successful it has been.

There are three main problems with the "better jobs" strategy. First, it is vague and unconvincing as a political message. If you are promising better jobs, I have no particular reason to believe that I will be one of the lucky few to get one. In other words, if I am struggling with medical bills or student loan payments, it's not clear how "ten million good jobs" will help me, even assuming that I believe you. Second, for the most part, the people facing the greatest economic challenges are precisely the people least able to get those high-skilled, high-paying jobs. If you are laid off from a factory in rural Ohio at the age of 50 with only a high school diploma, your chances of getting the education necessary to become a web designer, or a physical therapist, or a paralegal—let alone a software developer at Google—are pretty slim, as are the chances that companies will be recruiting for attractive positions in your area. Your difficulties are compounded by the fact that you have to find a way to support your family in the meantime, which probably means you will be forced to take low-wage jobs to get by. The same holds, albeit with less certainty, for children growing up in poor neighborhoods without stable housing, reliable nutrition, and good schools. The reality is that our society segments people into classes brutally and unfairly at birth and then uses the "free" labor market to maintain those divisions all the way through adulthood. Giving disadvantaged children even a faint chance against their better-housed, better-fed, better-schooled peers would require, at a minimum, the kind of sweeping health care, education, and housing solutions proposed above. Creating better jobs alone is not enough.

The third problem is that the "better jobs" story runs against the central macroeconomic transformation of our time. For a long time, the conventional wisdom was that technological process was good for people not only as consumers (because of lower prices) but also as workers. In the aggregate, people displaced from one industry would find new jobs elsewhere in the economy where they could be more productive. That was the case, by and large, for most of the Industrial Revolution; skilled weavers lost their jobs to automated looms, but their great-grandchildren became assembly-line workers in automobile and airplane factories. In recent decades, however, as those well-paid manufacturing jobs have been shipped overseas or eliminated through automation, the composition of the workforce has shifted toward low-paid service industry jobs. Although Silicon Valley, Wall Street, and the coastal media and entertainment hubs get most of the attention, in sheer numbers, job growth has come from food service, retail sales, caregiving, and other industries that rely on low-skilled labor. Right now, the occupations that are adding the most jobs are personal care aides, food preparation and serving workers, registered nurses, home health aides, restaurant cooks, software developers, and waiters and waitresses; five of those seven categories have typical annual wages below $27,000.[150] At Amazon, that shining icon of the new economy, the median salary in 2018 was only $35,000 in the United States, even after the company adopted a $15 minimum wage.[151]

In short, jobs are no longer shifting from low-productivity and low-wage occupations to high-productivity and high-wage ones. Technological progress in recent years has not resulted in overall employment losses, but it has reduced labor's share of overall income—that is, workers are getting a smaller slice of the economic pie.[152] Rising productivity in and of itself is not the problem. But when its benefits are monopolized by elite employees and shareholders, other workers are forced into lower-skill, lower-wage careers. Our economy continues to come up with new products and services, but today's hot industries, such as pharmaceuticals, media, and software, do not require enough skilled labor to absorb the people displaced from yesterday's leading sectors. At the extreme, Google and Facebook serve billions of customers with only a few tens of thousands of people. More generally, globalization and technology have enabled a small elite of highly educated, highly paid people to mobilize and oversee large armies of lower-skilled workers; Amazon's crack software developers, for example, write code that gives orders to hundreds of thousands of warehouse employees.

This dynamic may only get worse. Throughout history, when humans were replaced by technology, one reason most of us found better things to do is that we were always smarter than the machines. Today, however, machine learning is enabling computers to develop their own algorithms by analyzing large amounts of data with a minimal amount of human guidance. Computer programs are beginning to show the potential to master many of the types of cognitive tasks—recognizing patterns, drawing inferences, formulating and testing hypotheses, etc.—that are precisely what high-income humans are paid for. No one knows if or when computers will be able to displace the types of knowledge workers whose jobs have previously been immune to automation. But we already live in a world where economic progress no longer guarantees that children will have better job opportunities than their parents. We should by all means do what we can to help people find better work and higher pay. But focusing on "jobs" is not enough. We risk becoming a country where the large majority of our fellow Americans are stuck on the wrong side of a widening economic divide. It is incumbent on all of us to ensure that that does not happen.

The Myth of Trade-Offs

Any moderates who have made it this far will no doubt want to ask: How will you pay for all that? After all, fiscal responsibility, more than anything else, has been the hallmark economic position of establishment Democrats since the early days of the Clinton administration—the preferred way for politicians to signal "seriousness" and distinguish themselves from the dreaded specter of socialism.

On the one hand, this is an unfair question. The Bush tax cuts of 2001 and 2003 were not "paid for" by corresponding spending reductions, nor was the Trump tax cut of 2017—nor, for that matter, the Obama tax cuts of 2009 (stimulus bill), 2010 (first extension of the Bush tax cuts), and 2013 (permanent extension of most of the Bush tax cuts). So why is it that only progressive spending policies need to be paid for? Politically speaking, the answer is obvious: "Fiscal responsibility" has become little more than a catchphrase that moderates and conservatives use to criticize government programs that they don't like.

On the other hand, I do think that the long-term fiscal impact of new policies is something that should be considered. Higher deficits can certainly be warranted, particularly if they help counteract economic downturns (as in 2009) or if they make possible good long-term investments for the country (such as infrastructure or education). But sometimes, as was the case for the 2017 tax cut, they simply increase the national debt and hence our annual interest payments for no purpose whatsoever, squeezing out better uses of our collective resources.

For the issues above, the question is easily answered. Medicare for All can be funded by the money that companies and individuals already spend on health insurance premiums, deductibles, and co-payments. Because of Medicare's proven efficiency advantage and its superior ability to control costs, total health care spending should go down, which is what really matters at the end of the day. New construction of affordable housing units and expansion of the Section 8 program can be financed by eliminating or reducing existing tax breaks for homeowners such as the mortgage interest deduction. Social Security benefits can be expanded by applying the payroll tax to higher incomes and ending the tax preferences for retirement savings accounts that primarily benefit the affluent. That leaves only education, which could easily be justified as an investment in our nation's productive capacity (which will be paid back through higher tax revenues in the future) or paid for by a partial repeal of the 2017 tax cut.

Although all of the proposals above can be paid for, they will involve a shift in *who* pays. The financing for a single-payer health care system has to be explicitly progressive; otherwise lower-income people would be spending most of their wages on health insurance. The existing tax breaks for homeowners currently benefit the well-off; the housing programs that will replace them will help the poor and the middle class. The same is true of cutting tax deductions for retirement savings in favor of Social Security benefits. On balance, rich people will pay more to the federal government (and get less in housing and retirement subsidies), and poor and middle-class people will get more in the form of health insurance, education, lower rents, and retirement benefits.

But this is precisely the point. We should stop subsidizing the wealthy to do things they would do anyway (such as buying houses or saving money), and we should ensure that everyone has access to the basic necessities of modern life. Some may argue that asking high-earners to pay more will reduce their incentive to work and therefore undermine economic growth. For the most part, this is a red herring. Handouts hidden in the tax code, like the mortgage interest deduction, do not affect anyone's marginal incentive to work. To the extent that rich people will face higher tax rates, there is little evidence that this will have any effect on economic growth. (For more on this subject, see Chapter 5 of my earlier book, *Economism*.)

Even arguing about projected growth rates, however, falls prey to a rhetorical trap. All other things being equal, a larger economy is better than a smaller one. But right now, the problem is not growth; it's the unequal way that growth is being shared. From the end of 1979 through 2016, total output (GDP) per person increased by 82 percent.[153] For people in the bottom half of the income distribution, however, average pretax income—the amount they were able to earn from all sources, including Social Security and pensions—inched upward by only 2 percent, a rate of less than 0.1 percent per year. During the same period, their share of total pretax income fell from 21 percent to 13 percent.[154] In other words, if we could magically restore the level of inequality of 1979 (not a particularly egalitarian time, as I recall), the poorer half of the country would see their incomes rise by more than half. At a growth rate of less than 0.1 percent per year—what lower-income people have been able to gain from the market in recent decades—it would take literally hundreds of years to achieve a similar improvement in their economic fortunes.

Growth is not the answer. If we could squeeze another percentage point of increased production out of the economy, the large majority of those gains would be captured by the people who need them the least. Nor is "opportunity" a silver bullet. Even if we give the next generation slightly better skills to sell in the job market, the underlying problem is the highly unequal distribution of the spoils in our winner-take-all economy. Instead of repeating the dated slogans of an American dream that many people no longer believe in, we need to focus directly on the outcomes that matter: making sure that all people can live decent lives, even if they weren't born into affluent families and didn't go to good schools. That's what a good society does. And that's what it means to be the party of the people in 21st-century America.

Values

The economic agenda of our Democratic Party, as outlined above, is a concrete strategy to mitigate the inequality generated by contemporary capitalism and to address the pervasive insecurities faced by lower- and middle-income families. Our economic message is that we will fulfill the promise of a civilized society, one that shares the benefits of prosperity broadly and looks out for the needs of all of its members—that we will build a world in which no one has to worry about paying for health care, getting an education, finding a place to live, or saving enough for retirement. We will speak directly to the most immediate economic concerns of most American families. We will have a clear answer to Republicans who talk about small government and the magic of free markets: The purpose of an economy is not to generate an ever-increasing amount of stuff to be enjoyed by an ever-shrinking elite, but to provide for the basic welfare of all people.

Some people—particularly the centrist establishment of the Democratic Party—will call this a radical left-wing ideology. Some will call it socialism. Neither label is accurate. Socialism, if it means anything, means collective ownership of the productive resources of a society. Nothing suggested here encroaches on the basic structure of American capitalism.

The core principles of this economic platform are deeply ingrained in the spirit of our country. We have long prized not only rugged individualism, but also social solidarity and the duty to look out for our neighbors. For all of its flaws in practice, our nation was dedicated to the idea of a classless society, in which all people would enjoy equal rights and equal status—not an aristocracy of birth and privilege like the ones from which so many of our ancestors fled. We do not want to see our fellow citizens suffer from hunger, cold, or sickness. We do not want to see the elderly begging on the street. More than two-thirds of Americans believe that the government should ensure that "no one is without food, clothing, or shelter."[155] For better or for worse, for richer or for poorer, we are all one country, and it is our moral duty to look out for each other. Not every American will agree with our economic vision, yet it is a vision for all Americans.

The ethos of solidarity and shared prosperity is central to the historical identity of the Democratic Party. It motivated the finest hours of our history, when Franklin Roosevelt led the country out of the Great Depression and into World War II, and when Lyndon Johnson—despite his eventually disastrous mistakes—sought to make civil rights a reality and bring an end to poverty. "True individual freedom cannot exist without economic security and independence," Roosevelt said in 1944, as millions of Americans were fighting around the world. "We have accepted, so to speak, a second Bill of Rights under which a new basis of security and prosperity can be established for all regardless of station, race, or creed." These rights included: "The right of every family to a decent home; The right to adequate medical care and the opportunity to achieve and enjoy good health; The right to adequate protection from the economic fears of old age, sickness, accident, and unemployment; The right to a good education."[156]

This is the legacy that the Democratic establishment has rejected, and still rejects today. They do not believe, as Roosevelt did, that economic security is a fundamental right and an essential condition of a free society. The purpose of their Democratic Party is to foster private-sector growth, correct for market failures, help disadvantaged people gain more job skills—and then let the chips fall where they may.

Their Democratic Party has failed. It has failed to deliver the widespread prosperity that it promised; it has failed to stem the rise of extreme inequality; it has failed to maintain the trust of working- and middle-class voters; and it has failed to defend our democracy from the rise of bigotry, corruption, and authoritarianism, represented by President Trump and his Republican Party.

It is time for a change. It is time for the Democratic Party to stand for people, not for markets; for real security, not the empty promise of opportunity; for the 99 percent, not the 1 percent. It is time to take back our Democratic Party.

Acknowledgments

As with any endeavor, this book would not be in your hands today without the efforts of many people. Despite his more than full-time job as executive editor of *The American Prospect,* David Dayen agreed to edit the book and serialize it on the website of the *Prospect.* Susanna Beiser copy-edited the manuscript, and Jonathan Guyer chose the historical photos to illustrate the web version. Devin Hansen helped with online marketing. Ryan Grim agreed to publish the print edition at Strong Arm Press. Jordan Jones designed and typeset the interior, Soohee Cho created the cover, and Troy Miller managed production. This book tells a story and makes an argument, but neither would be possible without the work of the innumerable researchers and journalists who documented and analyzed the facts on which they are based. Finally, as always, I have enjoyed and relied on the love and friendship of my family.

Endnotes

1   Fabian T. Pfeffer and Robert F. Schoeni, "How Wealth Inequality Shapes Our Future," *The Russell Sage Foundation Journal of the Social Sciences* 2, no. 6 (October 2016): 2–22, p. 11.

2   Thomas Piketty, Emmanuel Saez, and Gabriel Zucman, "Distributional National Accounts: Methods and Estimates for the United States," *Quarterly Journal of Economics* 133, no. 2 (May 2018): 553–609, p. 578. After taxes and government spending, the effect is only slightly mitigated: income growth for the top 1% decreases from 204% to 194%, while income growth for the bottom 50% increases from 1% to 21%.

3   Ami Sedghi and George Arnett, "Will Your Generation Have a Better Life Than Your Parents?" *The Guardian*, April 14, 2014.

4   Daron Acemoglu and James A. Robinson, *Why Nations Fail: The Origins of Power, Prosperity, and Poverty* (Crown Business, 2012), pp. 152–56.

5   Quoted in "Conservative Advocate," *Morning Edition*, National Public Radio, May 25, 2001.

6   "What GOP fantasists imagine creating is a multicultural, identity-friendly party of capital. The problem is we already have such a party. Who needs two?" Corey Robin, "The Ruling-Class Circus," *Jacobin*, November 7, 2016.

7   Thomas Piketty, "Brahmin Left vs. Merchant Right: Rising Inequality and the Changing Structure of Political Conflict (Evidence from France, Britain and the US, 1948-2017)," WID.word Working Paper Series No. 2018/7.

8   Matthew Yglesias, "The Most Important Chart About the American Economy You'll See This Year," *Vox*, September 25, 2014.

9   William J. Clinton, "Address to the Democratic National Convention in Charlotte, North Carolina," September 5, 2012, The American Presidency Project, UC Santa Barbara.

10   "Democratic Leadership Council Keynote Address," May 6, 1991, C-SPAN.

11   Quoted in Kim Phillips-Fein, *Invisible Hands: The Businessmen's Crusade Against the New Deal* (W. W. Norton, 2009), p. 259.

12   Edward Cowan, "Democrats Offer New Policy to Sustain National Growth," *The New York Times*, September 19, 1982.

13   Thomas Ferguson and Joel Rogers, *Right Turn: The Decline of the Democrats and the Future of American Politics* (Macmillan, 1987), pp. 3–5.

14   Al From, *The New Democrats and the Return to Power* (Palgrave Macmillan, 2013), p. 50.

15   From, *The New Democrats and the Return to Power*, p. 2.

16   From, *The New Democrats and the Return to Power*, pp. 120–21.

17   Bill Clinton, *My Life* (Knopf, 2004), p. 326.

18   William J. Clinton, "Address Accepting the Presidential Nomination at the Democratic National Convention in New York," July 6, 1992, The American Presidency Project, UC Santa Barbara.

19   Bob Woodward, *The Agenda: Inside the Clinton White House* (Simon & Schuster, 1994), p. 73.

20 William Jefferson Clinton, "Address Before a Joint Session of the Congress on the State of the Union," January 23, 1996, The American Presidency Project, UC Santa Barbara.

21 Reihan Salam, "Normalizing Trade Relations With China Was a Mistake," *The Atlantic*, June 8, 2018; Justin R. Pierce and Peter K. Schott, "The Surprisingly Swift Decline of US Manufacturing Employment," *American Economic Review* 106, no. 7 (July 2016): 1632–62.

22 Quoted in From, *The New Democrats and the Return to Power*, p. 73.

23 Quoted in "Welfare Reform Working Group, Talking Points: Response to Charles Murray," May 3, 1994, Clinton Digital Library.

24 Peter Edelman, "The Worst Thing Bill Clinton Has Done," *The Atlantic*, March 1997.

25 Francis X. Clines, "Clinton Signs Bill Cutting Welfare; States in New Role," *The New York Times*, August 23, 1996.

26 Albert Gore, Jr., "Address Accepting the Presidential Nomination at the Democratic National Convention in Los Angeles," August 17, 2000, The American Presidency Project, UC Santa Barbara.

27 Barack Obama, "Keynote Address at the 2004 Democratic National Convention," July 27, 2004, The American Presidency Project, UC Santa Barbara.

28 Barack Obama, "Inaugural Address," January 20, 2009, The American Presidency Project, UC Santa Barbara.

29 Quoted in Eamon Javers, "Inside Obama's Bank CEOs Meeting," Politico, April 3, 2009.

30 Michael Grunwald, *The New New Deal: The Hidden Story of Change in the Obama Era* (Simon & Schuster, 2012), p. 97.

31 Reed Hundt, *A Crisis Wasted: Barack Obama's Defining Decisions* (Rosetta-Books, 2019), p. 107.

32 Hundt, *A Crisis Wasted*, p. 217.

33 Neil Barofsky, *Bailout: An Inside Account of How Washington Abandoned Main Street While Rescuing Wall Street* (Free Press, 2012), p. 156.

34   Laura Kusisto, "Many Who Lost Homes to Foreclosure in Last Decade Won't Return—NAR," *Wall Street Journal*, April 20, 2015.

35   Households; Owners' Equity in Real Estate, Level, FRED Economic Data, Federal Reserve Bank of St. Louis.

36   John Heilemann, "Obama Is from Mars, Wall Street Is from Venus," *New York*, May 22, 2010.

37   *Employer Health Benefits: 2019 Annual Survey*, Henry J. Kaiser Family Foundation, p. 7.

38   Health Insurance Historical Tables, U.S. Census Bureau, Table HIC-4.

39   Student Loans Owned and Securitized, Outstanding, FRED Economic Data, Federal Reserve Bank of St. Louis.

40   Miguel de Cervantes, *Don Quixote*, tr. J. M. Cohen (Collector's Library, 2006), 643.

41   Personal Income per Capita, FRED Economic Data, Federal Reserve Bank of St. Louis. Personal income includes realized income from all sources but excludes capital gains.

42   Alisha Coleman-Jensen, Matthew P. Rabbitt, Christian A. Gregory, and Anita Singh, Household Food Security in the United States in 2018, U.S. Department of Agriculture Economic Research Services, Report ERR-270 (September 2019), Table 1A.

43   Quoted in Al From, *The New Democrats and the Return to Power* (Palgrave Macmillan, 2013), p. 73.

44   Bill Clinton, Foreword to From, *The New Democrats and the Return to Power*.

45   Data from "The Productivity-Pay Gap," Economic Policy Institute, August 2018 (based on EPI analysis of data from Bureau of Labor Statistics and Bureau of Economic Analysis).

46   Data from Thomas Piketty, Emmanuel Saez, and Gabriel Zucman, "Distributional National Accounts: Methods and Estimates for the United States," *Quarterly Journal of Economics* 133, no. 2 (May 2018): 553-609, Appendix Table II-B3.

47 Data from Piketty, Saez, and Zucman, "Distributional National Accounts," Appendix Table II-B7b.

48 Piketty, Saez, and Zucman, "Distributional National Accounts," pp. 578–84, Appendix Table II-C3.

49 The Condition of Education 2015, National Center for Education Statistics, NCES 2015-144, May 2015, pp. 23, 27.

50 Fabian T. Pfeffer, "Growing Wealth Gaps in Education," *Demography* 55 (2018): 1033–68, Table 6.

51 Gabriel Zucman, "Global Wealth Inequality," *Annual Review of Economics* 11 (2019) (forthcoming).

52 Jonathan Rothbaum, "Median Earnings over the Last 40 Years," *Random Samplings*, U.S. Census Bureau, September 12, 2017.

53 Kayla Fontenot, Jessica Semega, and Melissa Kollar, Income and Poverty in the United States: 2018, U.S. Census Bureau Report No. P60-266, Table A-2.

54 Jonathan L. Rothbaum, "Highest Median Household Income on Record?" *America Counts: Stories Behind the Numbers*, U.S. Census Bureau, September 12, 2018.

55 Moritz Kuhn, Moritz Schularick, and Ulrike I. Steins, "Income and Wealth Inequality in America, 1949-2016," Federal Reserve Bank of Minneapolis, Opportunity & Inclusive Growth Institute Working Paper 9 (June 2018), p. 29.

56 Raj Chetty, David Grusky, Maximilian Hell, Nathaniel Hendren, Robert Manduca, and Jimmy Narang, "The Fading American Dream: Trends in Absolute Income Mobility Since 1940," *Science* 356, no. 6336 (April 28, 2017): 398–406, p. 398.

57 Robert A. Moffitt and Stephanie Garlow, "Did Welfare Reform Increase Employment and Reduce Poverty?" *Pathways* (Winter 2018): 17–21.

58 Robert Greenstein, "Welfare Reform and the Safety Net: Evidence Contradicts Likely Assumptions Behind Forthcoming GOP Poverty Plan," Center on Budget and Policy Priorities, June 6, 2016.

59   Jordan Weissmann, "The Failure of Welfare Reform," *Slate*, June 1, 2016.

60   H. Luke Shaefer and Kathryn Edin, "Welfare Reform and the Families It Left Behind," *Pathways* (Winter 2018): 22–27.

61   Kathryn J. Edin and H. Luke Shaefer, "Plasma Collections Hit All-Time High in 2014," *$2 a Day*, August 20, 2016.

62   Kathryn J. Edin and H. Luke Shaefer, "The Number of American Households Seeking Help at Food Pantries Hits Highest Point in Two Decades in 2014," *$2 a Day*, August 16, 2016.

63   Liz Schott, LaDonna Pavetti, and Ife Floyd, How States Use Federal and State Funds Under the TANF Block Grant, Center on Budget and Policy Priorities, October 15, 2015.

64   Ife Floyd, Ashley Burnside, and Liz Schott, "TANF Reaching Few Poor Families," Center on Budget and Policy Priorities, November 28, 2018.

65   Jared Bernstein, "This Is Your Safety Net on Block Grants," *On the Economy*, March 16, 2015.

66   2016 SCF Chartbook, Survey of Consumer Finances, Board of Governors of the Federal Reserve System, October 2017, p. 40

67   Renae Merle, "Wall Street's Average Bonus in 2017? Three Times What Most U.S. Households Made All Year," *The Washington Post*, March 26, 2018.

68   Annie Lowrey, "The Great Recession Is Still with Us," *The Atlantic*, December 1, 2017.

69   Homeownership Rate for the United States, FRED Economic Data, Federal Reserve Bank of St. Louis; *The State of the Nation's Housing 2018*, Joint Center for Housing Studies of Harvard University, 2018, p. 3.

70   *The State of the Nation's Housing 2018*, p. 5.

71   *2016 SCF Chartbook*, p. 40.

72   Bradley Sawyer and Cynthia Cox, "How Does Health Spending in the U.S. Compare to Other Countries?" *Peterson-Kaiser Health System Tracker*, December 7, 2018.

73 Rabah Kamal and Cynthia Cox, "How Has U.S. Spending on Healthcare Changed over Time?" *Peterson-Kaiser Health System Tracker*, December 10, 2018.

74 "Marketplace Average Benchmark Premiums," *State Health Facts*, Henry J. Kaiser Family Foundation.

75 *Employer Health Benefits: 2019 Annual Survey*, Henry J. Kaiser Family Foundation, p. 8.

76 *Employer Health Benefits: 2019 Annual Survey*, pp. 83, 122.

77 "Average Market Premiums Spike Across Obamacare Plans in 2018," *HealthPocket*, October 27, 2017.

78 Dan Witters, "U.S. Uninsured Rate Rises to Four-Year High," *Gallup*, January 23, 2019.

79 Health Insurance Marketplace Calculator, Henry J. Kaiser Family Foundation, October 31, 2019.

80 Sara R. Collins, Herman K. Bhupal, and Michelle M. Doty, *Health Insurance Coverage Eight Years After the ACA: Fewer Uninsured Americans and Shorter Coverage Gaps, But More Underinsured*, Survey Brief, The Commonwealth Fund, February 2019.

81 Sara R. Collins, Munira Z. Gunja, Michelle M. Doty, and Herman K. Bhupal, "Americans' Confidence in Their Ability to Pay for Health Care Is Falling," *To the Point*, The Commonwealth Fund, May 10, 2018.

82 Barack Obama, "Remarks at the Town Hall Education Arts Recreation Campus," December 4, 2018, The American Presidency Project, UC Santa Barbara.

83 "Public Opinion on Single-Payer, National Health Plans, and Expanding Access to Medicare Coverage," Henry J. Kaiser Family Foundation, June 19, 2019.

84 Mad Men, *The Monolith* (May 4, 2014).

85 Franklin D. Roosevelt, "Address at Madison Square Garden, New York City," October 31, 1936, The American Presidency Project, UC Santa Barbara.

86   State Partisan Composition, National Conference of State Legislatures.

87   Katie Reilly, "Read Hillary Clinton's Speech Attacking Donald Trump's Economic Policies," *Time*, June 22, 2016.

88   Chuck Schumer, "A Better Deal for American Workers," *The New York Times*, July 24, 2017.

89   This American Life, *I Thought It Would Be Easier* (January 19, 2018).

90   Civilian Unemployment Rate, FRED Economic Data, Federal Reserve Bank of St. Louis.

91   Total Unemployed, Plus All Marginally Attached Workers Plus Total Employed Part Time for Economic Reasons, FRED Economic Data, Federal Reserve Bank of St. Louis.

92   Richard K. Armey, *The Freedom Revolution: The New Republican Majority Leader Tells Why Big Government Failed, Why Freedom Works, and How We Will Rebuild America* (Regnery, 1995), p. 316.

93   Lisa Friedman, "Dianne Feinstein Lectures Children Who Want Green New Deal, Portraying It as Untenable," *The New York Times*, February 22, 2019.

94   Rahm Emanuel, "How Not to Lose to Donald Trump," *The Atlantic*, March 10, 2019.

95   Shane Goldmacher and Jonathan Martin, "2020 Democrats Love Small Donors. But Some Really Love Big Donors, Too," *The New York Times*, March 30, 2019; Tory Newmyer, "The Finance 202: Buttigieg Breaks Out—with Wall Street Donors," *The Washington Post*, November 6, 2019.

96   Albert Gore, Jr., "Address Accepting the Presidential Nomination at the Democratic National Convention in Los Angeles," August 17, 2000, The American Presidency Project, UC Santa Barbara.

97   Jon Huang, Samuel Jacoby, Michael Strickland, and K. K. Rebecca Lai, "Election 2016: Exit Polls," *The New York Times*, November 8, 2016.

98   Shannon M. Monnat and David L. Brown, "More Than a Rural Revolt: Landscapes of Despair and the 2016 Presidential Election," *Journal of Rural Studies* 55 (2017): 227–36, pp. 231–32.

99   Thomas Ferguson, Benjamin Page, Jacob Rothschild, Arturo Chang, and Jie Chen, "The Economic and Social Roots of Populist Rebellion: Support for Donald Trump in 2016," Institute for New Economic Thinking Working Paper No. 83 (October 2018), p. 40.

100   David Autor, David Dorn, Gordon Hanson, and Kaveh Majlesi, "A Note on the Effect of Rising Trade Exposure on the 2016 Presidential Election" (March 2, 2017), Appendix to David Autor, David Dorn, Gordon Hanson, and Kaveh Majlesi "Importing Political Polarization? The Electoral Consequences of Rising Trade Exposure," MIT working paper (December 2017).

101   Thomas Piketty, "Brahmin Left vs. Merchant Right: Rising Inequality & the Changing Structure of Political Conflict (Evidence from France, Britain and the US, 1948-2017)," WID.world Working Paper Series No. 2018/7, Figure 3.4c.

102   Sheera Frenkel, Nicholas Confessore, Cecilia Kang, Matthew Rosenberg, and Jack Nicas, "Delay, Deny and Deflect: How Facebook's Leaders Fought Through Crisis," *New York Times*, November 14, 2018.

103   Dwight D. Eisenhower, Letter to Edgar Newton Eisenhower, November 8, 1954, in Louis Galambos and Daun Van Ee, eds., *The Papers of Dwight David Eisenhower*, doc. 1147 (Johns Hopkins University Press, 1996).

104   Quoted in Thomas B. Edsall, "Jackson, Robb Tussle over Democratic Strategy," *The Washington Post*, March 11, 1989.

105   *America's Resilient Center and the Road to 2020: Results from a New National Survey*, Progressive Policy Institute and Expedition Strategies, 2018; Ronald Brownstein, "A Referendum on America's Identity," *The Atlantic*, July 13, 2016.

106 *2016 SCF Chartbook*, Survey of Consumer Finances, Board of Governors of the Federal Reserve System (last updated October 16, 2017), pp. 115, 835, 838.

107 *The Precarious State of Family Balance Sheets*, The Pew Charitable Trusts, January 2015.

108 Jacob S. Hacker, Philipp Rehm and Mark Schlesinger, "The Insecure American: Economic Experiences, Financial Worries, and Policy Attitudes," *Perspectives on Politics* 11, no. 1 (March 2013): 23–49, p. 27.

109 *Report on the Economic Well-Being of U.S. Households in 2018*, Board of Governors of the Federal Reserve System, May 2019, pp. 2, 4.

110 Jacob S. Hacker, *The Great Risk Shift: The New Economic Insecurity and the Decline of the American Dream*, 2nd edition (Oxford University), pp. 22–27; Jacob S. Hacker, Gregory A. Huber, Austin Nichols, Philipp Rehm, Mark Schlesinger, Rob Valletta, and Stuart Craig, "The Economic Security Index: A New Measure for Research and Policy Analysis," *The Review of Income and Wealth* 60, Supplement (March 2014): S5–32.

111 Hacker, Rehm and Schlesinger, "The Insecure American," pp. 36–41.

112 Katharine Bradbury, "Levels and Trends in the Income Mobility of U.S. Families, 1977–2012," Federal Reserve Bank of Boston Working Paper 16-8 (2016). Bradbury looks at intragenerational income mobility for families headed by working-age adults. Measures of intergenerational mobility (comparing parents and children) have remained relatively stable over this period (and lower than in most other comparable countries). Raj Chetty, Nathaniel Hendren, Patrick Kline, and Emmanuel Saez, "Where Is the Land of Opportunity? The Geography of Intergenerational Mobility in the United States," *Quarterly Journal of Economics* 129, no. 4 (2014): 1553-1623.

113 Stanley Greenberg, "How She Lost" (review of Amie Parnes and Jonathan Allen, *Shattered: Inside Hillary Clinton's Doomed Campaign*), *The American Prospect*, Fall 2017.

114   Letitia Stein, Susan Cornwell, and Joseph Tanfani, "Inside the Progressive Movement Roiling the Democratic Party," *Reuters*, August 23, 2018.

115   "Public Opinion on Single-Payer, National Health Plans, and Expanding Access to Medicare Coverage," Henry J. Kaiser Family Foundation, June 19, 2019.

116   Ben Casselman and Jim Tankersley, "Warren Wealth Tax Has Wide Support, Except Among One Group," *The New York Times*, November 29, 2019.

117   David Dayen, "The Medicare for All Cost Debate Is Extremely Dishonest," *The American Prospect*, October 22, 2019.

118   James J. Heckman, Seong Hyeok Moon, Rodrigo Pinto, Peter A. Savelyev, and Adam Yavitz, "The Rate of Return to the HighScope Perry Preschool Program," *Journal of Public Economics* 94 (2010): 114–28.

119   Allison Friedman-Krauss, W. Steven Barnett, and Milagros Nores, *How Much Can High-Quality Universal Pre-K Reduce Achievement Gaps?*, Center for American Progress and National Institute for Early Education Research (April 2016), p. 4.

120   Emma Garcia, *Inequalities at the Starting Gate: Cognitive and Noncognitive Skills Gaps between 2010–2011 Kindergarten Classmates*, Economic Policy Institute (June 17, 2015), p. 9.

121   W. Steven Barnett and Donald J. Yarosz, *Who Goes to Preschool and Why Does It Matter?*, National Institute for Early Education Research Preschool Policy Brief (November 2007), p. 7.

122   Friedman-Krauss, Barnett, and Nores, *How Much Can High-Quality Universal Pre-K Reduce Achievement Gaps?*, p. 12.

123   Ben Miller, "The Student Debt Problem Is Worse Than We Imagined," *The New York Times*, August 25, 2018.

124   Ella Nilson, "Progressives Want to Go Further Than Tuition-Free College—Here's Their Proposal to Make It Debt-Free," *Vox*, March 7, 2019.

125   Ronald Brownstein, "What Do Americans Think About Access to Education?" *The Atlantic*, March 9, 2016; Benjamin I. Page, Larry M. Bartels,

and Jason Seawright, "Democracy and the Policy Preferences of Wealthy Americans," *Perspectives on Politics* 11, no. 1 (March 2013): 51–73, p. 59.

126 Page, Bartels, and Seawright, "Democracy and the Policy Preferences of Wealthy Americans," p. 59; Martha C. White, "Two-Thirds of Americans Support Free College Tuition," *NBC News*, August 1, 2016; "Strong Support For Policies That Address The College Affordability Crisis, New Study Shows" (press release), Demos, March 14, 2018.

127 See Nick Hanauer, "Better Public Schools Won't Fix America," *The Atlantic*, July 2019.

128 Matthew Desmond, "How Homeownership Became the Engine of American Inequality," *The New York Times Magazine*, May 9, 2017.

129 Consumer Price Index for All Urban Consumers: Rent of Primary Residence, FRED Economic Data, Federal Reserve Bank of St. Louis; Consumer Price Index for All Urban Consumers: All Items, FRED Economic Data, Federal Reserve Bank of St. Louis.

130 *The State of the Nation's Housing 2018*, Joint Center for Housing Studies of Harvard University, 2018, pp. 5, 30.

131 Liza Getsinger, Lily Posey, Graham MacDonald, Josh Leopold, and Katya Abazajian, "The Housing Affordability Gap for Extremely Low-Income Renters in 2014," Urban Institute, April 2017.

132 *The State of the Nation's Housing 2018*, p. 34.

133 Peter Dreier, "Why America Needs More Social Housing," *The American Prospect*, April 16, 2018; Peter Gowan and Ryan Cooper, *Social Housing in the United States*, People's Policy Project (2018).

134 *The State of the Nation's Housing 2018*, p. 33.

135 *The State of the Nation's Housing 2018*, pp. 32–33.

136 *Estimates of Federal Tax Expenditures for Fiscal Years 2018–2022*, Joint Committee on Taxation, JCX-81-18 (October 4, 2018), Tables 1 and 2.

137 Dora L. Costa, *The Evolution of Retirement: An American Economic History, 1880–1990* (University of Chicago, 1998), p. 8; Felicitie C. Bell and Michael L. Miller, *Life Tables for the United States Social Security Area*

1900-2100, Social Security Administration Actuarial Study No. 120, August 2005.

138 *2016 SCF Chartbook*, Survey of Consumer Finances, Board of Governors of the Federal Reserve System, October 2017, pp. 441–42.

139 Alicia H. Munnell, Wenliang Hou, and Geoffrey T. Sanzenbacher, "National Retirement Risk Index Shows Modest Improvement in 2016," Center for Retirement Research at Boston College, Number 18-1, January 2018.

140 Paul N. Van de Water and Kathy Ruffing, *Social Security Benefits Are Modest*, Center on Budget and Policy Priorities, August 7, 2017; "Monthly Statistical Snapshot, October 2019," Social Security, November 2019; Michael Clingman, Kyle Burkhalter, and Chris Chaplain, "Replacement Rates for Hypothetical Retired Workers," Social Security Administration Actuarial Note Number 2019.9, April 2019, Table C.

141 *The Distribution of Major Tax Expenditures in the Individual Income Tax System*, Congressional Budget Office, May 2013.

142 *Estimates of Federal Tax Expenditures for Fiscal Years 2018–2022*, Table 1.

143 *America's Resilient Center and the Road to 2020*, Progressive Policy Institute and Expedition Strategies; *National Survey Results*, Public Policy Polling, March 9–11, 2018.

144 "Social Security," *Gallup* (question asked in 2005 and 2010).

145 Civilian Unemployment Rate, FRED Economic Data, Federal Reserve Bank of St. Louis; Total Unemployed, Plus All Marginally Attached Workers Plus Total Employed Part Time for Economic Reasons, FRED Economic Data, Federal Reserve Bank of St. Louis.

146 National Occupational Employment and Wage Estimates, Bureau of Labor Statistics, May 2018.

147 *Few Rewards: An Agenda to Give America's Working Poor a Raise*, Oxfam America and Economic Policy Institute, June 2016, p. 3; Poverty Thresholds (2018), U.S. Census Bureau.

148 50th Percentile Rent Estimates (2019), Office of Policy Development and Research, U.S. Department of Housing and Urban Development.

149   Union Membership, Bureau of Labor Statistics Economic News Release, January 18, 2019, Table 3: Union Affiliation of Employed Wage and Salary Workers by Occupation and Industry.

150   Employment Projections, Bureau of Labor Statistics, September 4, 2019, Table 1.4: Occupations with the Most Job Growth, 2018 and Projected 2028.

151   Benjamin Romano, "Amazon Reveals What Typical U.S. Worker Makes After Its Minimum-Wage Bump," *The Seattle Times*, April 11, 2019.

152   David Autor and Anna Salomons, "Is Automation Labor-Displacing? Productivity Growth, Employment, and the Labor Share," *Brookings Papers on Economic Activity*, Spring 2018.

153   Real Gross Domestic Product per Capita, FRED Economic Data, Federal Reserve Bank of St. Louis.

154   Thomas Piketty, Emmanuel Saez, and Gabriel Zucman, "Distributional National Accounts: Methods and Estimates for the United States," *Quarterly Journal of Economics* 133, no. 2 (May 2018), Appendix Tables II-B1, II-B3. I chose 2016 as the ending date because it is the last year included in the latest data series provided by Piketty, Saez, and Zucman, the most comprehensive source of estimates of the distribution of income and wealth for the United States.

155   Page, Bartels, and Seawright, "Democracy and the Policy Preferences of Wealthy Americans." In addition, more than 40% of Americans believe that the maxim "From each according to his ability, to each according to his needs"—actually from *The Communist Manifesto* by Karl Marx and Friedrich Engels—is in the U.S. Constitution or another of our country's founding documents. Katelyn Sills, "Do You Think Teens Know the Difference Between Madison and Marx?" Bill of Rights Institute.

156   Franklin D. Roosevelt, "State of the Union Message to Congress," January 11, 1944, The American Presidency Project, UC Santa Barbara.

Index

D

E

P

Patient Protection and Affordable Care Act of 2010. See Affordable
Care Act

Perot, Ross 59

Personal Responsibility and Work Opportunity Reconciliation Act of
1996 19, 47

Pocan, Mark 89

Progressive Policy Institute

    a think tank spun off from the DLC 13

    Democratic think tank supporting market-based solutions 25

    Robert Shapiro moves to 1992 Clinton campaign 14

R

redistribution

    and Social Security and Medicare 40

Reece, Florence 1

Reed, Bruce 14

Republican Party

    transformation by radical conservatives 5

Riegle-Neal Act of 1994 22

Robb, Charles

    Coalition for a Democratic Majority rejects New Deal 13

Robinson, James 4

Roosevelt, Franklin

    1933, shut bankers out of inner circle 30

    1936 speech on enemies 60

    creation of Social Security 10

    Democratic heritage 5

    DLC repudiation of populist economic agenda 13

    economic security 60

    established federal safety net 5

About the Author

James Kwak is a professor at the UConn School of Law and the chair of the board of the Southern Center for Human Rights. He is the author or co-author of three previous books: *13 Bankers* (a *New York Times* bestseller), *White House Burning,* and *Economism.* Prior to going to law school, he co-founded Guidewire Software. James has an A.B. in social studies from Harvard College, a Ph.D. in history from the University of California, Berkeley, and a J.D. from the Yale Law School. He lives in Amherst, Massachusetts, with his wife and two children.

CPSIA information can be obtained
at www.ICGtesting.com
Printed in the USA
LVHW091602250220
648164LV00005B/887

9 781947 492431